The Last Years of British Rail
1980-84

The Last Years of British Rail 1980-84

John Stretton

· BRITISH RAILWAYS COLLECTION ·

from

The NOSTALGIA Collection

First published by Silver Link Publishing as part of *Closely Observed Trains* in 1994
This edition first published 2004

British Library Cataloguing in Publication Data

A catalogue record for this book is available from the British Library.

ISBN 1 85794 215 9

Silver Link Publishing Ltd
The Trundle
Ringstead Road
Great Addington
Kettering
Northants NN14 4BW

Tel/Fax: 01536 330588
email: sales@nostalgiacollection.com
Website: www.nostalgiacollection.com

Printed and bound in Great Britain

Frontispiece I make no apologies for reprising this picture; seen in *Closely Observed Trains* as part of the 1980 selection, this is a classic example of why the photographer is a renowned and recognised expert in the field of modern railway photography. How many of us, I wonder, would have thought of waiting to capture this Gloucester Class 119 unit at this precise point, as it leaves Penwithers Junction, south of Truro, on 4 July 1980, forming the 1410 Truro-Falmouth service? As well as making a compelling image, it also serves to emphasis the loneliness of the branch line, compared to the freshly ballasted main line in the foreground. *Brian Morrison*

Acknowledgements

A s with the other two volumes in this series of books, I am indebted to the small coterie of photographers who have helped me with the project. They are basically the same four that assisted me with the compilation of *Closely Observed Trains*, which looked at BR in the 1980s and from which this new edition has been carved. Their continued co-operation, assistance, support and encouragement is valued more than they are aware. I am also grateful to the publishers for the loan of some of Ray Ruffell's photographs from their library. In addition, my heartfelt thanks go to Brian Morrison for his efforts in proof-reading and coping with the slight incompatibilities between his electronic system and mine! How he managed to fit it all in between trips to Germany, various parts of the UK and the USA, I shall never know. The illustrations with a credit 'MJS' are mine. As usual, credit and huge thanks must go to my wife Judi, who tolerates long periods of isolation, or me like a bear with a sore head, as I either sit huddled gnome-like in front of the computer or peer at innumerable photographs. Without her continued forbearance, I could not have achieved the task within the deadline! Finally, thanks to Peter Townsend at Silver Link for encouragement and putting up with countless phone calls; to David in the Silver Link office for his unflinching patience and courtesy; and to Mick and Will for their usual skilful and speedy editing and design. Thank you all!

Contents

Enthusiasts are often accused of an obsessive devotion to their hobby and, certainly, as the years have passed, followers of certain types of motive power have lavished much affection on their subjects, but how many would stand in humble reverence and pray in this fashion…? Hushed surroundings at Liverpool Street envelop this devotee 'worshipping' No 47422 as it stands between duties on 22 April 1983. *MJS*

Introduction

Let me state at the outset that this volume is a child of *Closely Observed Trains*, published by Silver Link in 1994 but now long out of print. However, while some of the illustrations in this latest book may be familiar, there are, equally, many new ones, as the opportunity has been taken to split that original into two and to update and revise the previous captions. Much has happened over the past ten years that has changed the story of the five years covered herein, not least in the developments and changes in fortune of the various classes of motive power. Wherever possible I have attempted to bring the story up to date with the benefit of added hindsight since preparing the original book. The third volume, published first, covers the years 1990-94, and the second the years 1985-89.

When the half-decade covered by this current volume dawned – incredibly, now 20-plus years ago – we had endured a little over a decade since the demise of steam on BR metals and were emerging from what is now lovingly referred to as the 'Blue Period'. There had been changes in numbering, with the introduction of TOPS, the HSTs had arrived and had made their mark on the ex-GWR main lines, and there had been some departures of both locomotives and routes/stations served, but, in retrospect, it was a quiet time. However, that was to change. Politically, as well as on the railways, there were disturbances and ideas under the surface that would burst forth as the decade wore on, and the former certainly had an effect on the latter!

Margaret Thatcher's antipathy to railways is now well known, but in 1980 that was all to come.

This volume covers the demise of the 'Deltics', the expulsion of 'Peaks' from Midland Main Line front-line services, the end of the Class 40s and the Woodhead route, and many other slightly less cataclysmic events. Viewed from a 21st-century vantage point, the threats and dubious statistic-manipulating that accompanied the proposals for both the Settle-Carlisle and Marylebone routes seem suicidal, and it is to the credit of all concerned in the protests at the time that those two areas were saved. Sadly, the 'Leicester Gap' was not protected, and we see the last days of signals and infrastructure in this book.

While this five-year period was probably the quietest of the 15 covered by this series, there is still much to see and enjoy, and certainly many images and views that can no longer be so enjoyed. It is easy to view such images through rosy spectacles and wallow in questionable nostalgia, but in this case it is both valid and necessary to see what we have lost and appreciate its value, possibly to take up the cudgels in future to prevent similar, unworthy wholesale slaughter. I have thoroughly enjoyed 'going back in time' in the preparation of this volume and I hope you, dear reader, will be likewise nourished and satisfied as you browse through these wonderful images! They have been chosen for their aesthetic quality, as well as their historic value, and have come from the cameras of some of the country's leading exponents of the art. Enjoy.

One of the many railway delights that I have enjoyed over the years is being by the line out in the countryside on a warm summer's day, relaxing in the peace and quiet of rural surroundings. One such occasion was 6 June 1983, at Hyde Heath on the northern approach to Amersham on the former Met&GC line from Aylesbury. It was a humdrum scene at the time, but one that is now imbued with nostalgia for a period long gone and for motive power that has become fondly remembered following its disappearance. A Class 115 DMU set heads towards the Amersham stop with a late-morning Aylesbury-Marylebone service. *MJS*

Classic photographers such as Colin Gifford, Eric Treacy and Brian Morrison have long espoused a departure from the standard front-three-quarter view. As will be seen elsewhere in this volume, the adoption of a vantage point higher or lower than the norm often enhances the view, but it still takes a brave soul to move away from the 'accepted wisdom' as seen in so many books and periodicals. On 16 June 1984 this photographer has cleverly employed a vertical format together with framing by the station canopy and parcels trolleys to present an attractive portrait of No 33032 about to leave Crewe with the 1600 'cross-country' service to Cardiff. *Tom Heavyside*

1980

4 March

As the decade dawned, quietly after the 'blue years' of the 1970s, none of us could have foreseen the massive amount of change that would be wrought on our railways. It scarcely seemed feasible that the 'Deltics' would disappear within two years, or that, progressively, other types would follow, suddenly acquiring their own acolytes as they approached extinction from the main line. The Class 50s would end this decade much loved, but in 1980, although of interest in view of only recently having been transferred to the WR from the WCML, they were still relatively unsung. With Reading's skyline behind, No 50006 *Neptune* heads west past Southcote Junction with the 1230 Paddington-Plymouth train, still in blue four months after refurbishment and naming. Its end came in 1987. *Colin Marsden*

◄ 7 March

After mention of the 'Deltics', here is one of the class – No 55022 *Royal Scots Grey*, the pioneer despite its number – arriving at Newcastle at the head of a 'stopper', the 1425 from Edinburgh, already something of a come-down to the past glories of handling the prestigious ECML expresses after the ousting of Gresley's 'A4s' some 20 years earlier. Withdrawn from service on 2 January 1982, concurrently with the other three final survivors, the engine was happily saved for preservation and restoration to its original livery. *Tom Heavyside*

◄ 10 April

Another '50', but this time featuring on the Waterloo-Exeter route, where the class saw out its last days of front-line service. While many preferred either the large-numbered livery of the mid-1980s or the 'Network SouthEast' 'raspberry ripple' that came later, the more subtle, toned-down earlier blue version, with yellow front end and cab surrounds, was not unattractive and is seen here on No 50042 *Triumph*, passing Surbiton on the last stages of its journey to the metropolis with the 0615 Exeter-Waterloo service. Once again, as in the Frontispiece, the photographer has gained both height and advantage to capture this pleasing image, setting the train within its context. *Colin Marsden*

▲ 13 April

Growing up near the Midland main line, north of Leicester, the Class 44s, 45s and 46s – or 'Peaks' to us older spotters – held a special place in my affections, but to the wider audience they went about their business largely unnoticed, although their time was to come within two years, as HSTs promised to wipe them from the face of the earth from September 1982. As Type 4 mixed-traffic locomotives, their geographical travels were far and wide, with all manner of consists, both passenger and freight. Here No 45039 *The Manchester Regiment* drives past Chepstow on an early Sunday morning Cardiff-Portsmouth Harbour service. *Brian Morrison*

▲ 23 April

How to make a mundane scene more interesting. The 1610 Hexham-Newcastle service, comprising a Cravens Class 105 twin-car DMU set led by E56474, pauses at Wylam, on the Northumberland border, framed by the latticed footbridge and the magnificent signal box gantry. Fifteen months later this unit was refitted as a Sandite Unit, under Departmental identity ADB 977049; it had disappeared from active duty by the end of the decade. *Tom Heavyside*

▼ 26 April

The Settle-Carlisle route spent much of the period of this volume in the news, threatened by the powers that be in British Rail trying desperately to close it, while literally thousands of supporters – railway enthusiasts and ordinary public alike – fought their corner to save it. Fortunately it survived long enough, despite 'lies, damned lies and distorted statistics', with the help of that determined opposition, to see a shift in public opinion regarding railways and become an idea that met its time. Before all this – and the deliberate re-routing of traffic away from the line – No 47535 enjoys the sunshine in the magnificent scenery around Ais Gill as it powers the 0952 Leicester-Glasgow service northwards. *Tom Heavyside*

▲ 28 April

One more level crossing about to hit the headlines? Thankfully not, as the Vauxhall, the aspect foreshortened by a telephoto lens, is in no imminent danger as No 47706 *Strathclyde* is stopped at the signal, west of Falkirk, at the point where the ex-North British Railway crosses the Forth & Clyde Canal, while working the 1005 Glasgow-Edinburgh service, diverted on this occasion via Falkirk Grahamston due to the temporary closure of Falkirk High tunnel. One hopes that the flat-capped signalman appreciates this extra work, encamped in his 1899-vintage ex-NBR 'non-standard' Swing Bridge East box. *Tom Noble*

▼ 26 May

There are many elements that go to make up an attractive picture, and here it is the gathering and position of the onlookers that make this shot so successful. To recognise and celebrate the 150th anniversary of various parts of our railway system, BR organised several events. Among the most enjoyable, by virtue of the many ancient locos taking part, were the Rocket 150 celebrations. Here, ex-LNWR 2-4-0 No 790 *Hardwicke* enjoys its '15 minutes of fame' and the many admiring glances as it leaves Bold Colliery and passes through St Helens Junction station, en route to the day's cavalcade. *Tom Heavyside*

▲ 27 May

What so many of us realised only in retrospect – often when it was way too late – was how much of the long-established railway scene was disappearing under our very noses. Having been there for generations, it seemed so permanent, but sadly not so. Some of the rationalisation at Bishop Auckland can be glimpsed in this view of a Cravens twin-car DMU unit (comprising E51482 and E56423) as it waits to form the 1510 service to Darlington. In happier times a web of lines radiated from the town and, until August 1968, those seen here would have continued to Durham, but now some of the ex-NER station's structures have been stripped from the Durham platform, as well as the middle tracks, and the whole has a feeling of dilapidation. Only the surviving semaphores and the deceptively substantial signal box hark back to halcyon days. *Brian Morrison*

▼ 29 May

This classic location and vantage point never palled either in steam days or even up to this period of BR; however, there were to be dramatic changes as the decade progressed, with rationalisation of the left-hand layout and the abandonment of the right-hand platforms! The diamond crossing is no more and cars now occupy the former platforms 1-6 area, including where the DMU stands on the right of this delightful view. Alas, Class 40s are also just a memory in everyday service, now limited to one or two preserved lines and the very occasional outing on the main line. On this day No 40073, with route discs removed, heads north through Newcastle with an ammonia train. *Brian Morrison*

18 June

More abandonment is seen here at Alloa East, as No 20218 threads a westbound coal train through the depressing-looking station site. Like Bishop Auckland just seen, Alloa was once at the centre of a whole network of routes, of both North British and Caledonian origin, but progressively, from the 1960s, parts of the web were stripped away. The station is closed and some ripping up of tracks in the goods yard area can be seen on the right. However, there are currently plans to construct a new station in Alloa town centre and operate passenger services again between Alloa, Stirling and Glasgow (Queen Street). In hindsight, the view of a single Class 20 on a freight is something to savour. Built as D8318 in November 1967 and allocated to Haymarket, it assumed the number 20218 in September 1974 and worked much of its life in Scotland, before moving south and finally being withdrawn from Toton in October 1989. *Tom Heavyside*

19 June

We have already seen the advantage of an elevated vantage point, but another vital aspect of successful modern railway photography is an eye for the telling detail. In this case, as well as placing the train strategically on the 'golden third', the photographer has chosen a vertical format to fully encompass and highlight the sinuous curves on the northern exit from Dawlish. Seemingly ignored by the elderly couple strolling along the seafront, No 25058 has a relatively easy task,

leaning into the curve with its short rake of just five coaches, forming the 1125 Paignton-Exeter stopper. Built at BR Derby in June 1963, as D5208, its initial allocation was local, to Toton. Renumbered 25058 in February 1974, it succumbed to the inevitable from Crewe Diesel Depot on 3 February 1987 and was cut up at Vic Berry's Leicester site in December 1988, but not before having been graced with *Castell Criccieth/Criccieth Castle* nameplates at Aberystwyth. *Colin Marsden*

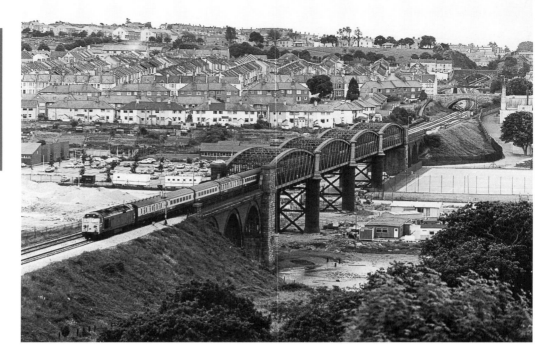

▲ 20 June

A trap that so many photographers fall into – including your author too often in the past! – is to go for a close-up view, ignoring the context in which the subject matter sits. As well as yet another elevated view, the photographer has here overcome that temptation and has transformed an otherwise 'bog standard' shot into one of power and impact by retreating to encompass the panorama. No 50049 *Defiance* – last of the class to be built, in December 1968 – crosses the delightful four-span metal viaduct at St Budeaux, on freshly ballasted track, at the head of the 1330 Paddington-Penzance service. Named at Laira depot on 2 May 1978, No 50049 obtained some notoriety by being renumbered to 50149 between 9 August 1987 and 22 February 1989. It was withdrawn on 16 August 1991. *Colin Marsden*

▼ 22 June

Another '50', but one employed on a different consist. Crossing the short but highly attractive stone viaduct at Liskeard, No 50012 *Benbow* powers northwards as the 1640 St Austell-Kensington Motorail service. An excellent idea, to transport driver and car by rail over the long distance up to London, it was tragically not to be an unbounded success and the rug was pulled later in the decade. *Colin Marsden*

▲ 26 July

Together with routes such as the Settle-Carlisle line, many branch lines have seen repeated rumours of and/or efforts to effect closure. One that has seemingly hung on by its fingernails is the Middlesbrough-Whitby branch. Passing though sparsely populated countryside, the economics of providing a social service have weighed against it with the 'bean-counters'. Happily it has survived and, in the 21st century, there seems to be a final recognition that time and money should be spent on the route and its advertising. In the days of 'first generation' DMUs, a Metro-Cammell Class 101 forms the 1757 Middlesbrough-Whitby local and waits at Glaisdale – a passing loop station on the largely single-line branch – for the 1831 reverse service to arrive. *MJS collection*

▼ 16 August

We have seen clever framing from this photographer before, but here he has used the bridge parapet at Weeton, between Singleton and Kirkham, that would probably have been excluded by most, to provide an L-shaped surround for No 47435 as it heads the 1820 Blackpool North-Euston train. Emerging from Crewe Works in February 1964, as D1550 – the first of the 'Brush 4s' to be built at Crewe – its initial allocation was to Sheffield (Darnall) on the ER. Becoming No 47435 exactly 11 years later, withdrawal came on 15 March 1990, from Crewe Diesel Depot; it was later to travel to Booth-Roe's scrapyard in Rotherham, where it was cut up in December 1993. *Tom Heavyside*

▲ 16 August

Another humble twin-car DMU set (here comprising M56224 and M50976) and more dereliction: presumably economic considerations have determined some retrenchment in the former Lytham station buildings to the left, as there is clear evidence of the removal of platform canopies, the windows are boarded, and the brickwork is now fenced off and providing home to greenery. However, the footbridge indicates that the down platform is still open to passengers. The train is the 1928 Blackpool South-Kirkham local stopper, which would have been an easy duty for this set. *Tom Heavyside*

▼ 21 August

Here is another view, unremarkable at the time, that has gained power and interest with age! Class 50-hauled front-line services were an everyday occurrence in Devon at this time, but not so by the end of the decade, when all such services were in the hands of HSTs. No 50016 *Barham* just managed to see out the decade, being stopped in 1990 with power unit problems and formally withdrawn on 10 July, but here it is in full throat, with exhaust shimmering above the loco's body as it rounds the curve at Aller Junction with the 1130 Penzance-bound train from London. *Colin Marsden*

▲ 4 September

The bold, daring and highly decorative ex-LNWR fan-tail window at Buxton – once with a twin at the long extinct ex-Midland station next door – still commands attention, bare and exposed at the end of the terminal platforms, a tribute to its original designer. The work of the co-ordinated mail employees was also a tribute to just one aspect of the huge variety of business once handled by Britain's railways. Sadly, in 2003/4 Royal Mail saw fit to jettison this revenue source and the rail mailbags have gone the same way as the non-gangwayed Class 128 DPU No 55990 seen here being loaded. Built in January 1960, it travelled to East Anglia just over 18 months after this view, in April 1982, to be cut up at Mayer Newman's, Snailwell, within the month. *Brian Morrison*

▼ 6 September

As the decade opened there was certainly no general thought of the 'Peaks' disappearing from the scene. Even when the HSTs assumed the mantle on the Midland main line, there were plans to transfer them to other duties and even prepare them to run well into the 1990s. Sadly, a reversal of thought brought the end ever closer as the 1980s rolled by. In much happier times, and most definitely retaining its character, with the split-headcode boxes, a smart-looking No 45120 passes Dronfield, prior to the station's re-opening, at the head of the 1010 Sheffield-St Pancras express, having just emerged from Broadway Tunnel. *Brian Morrison*

▲ 6 September

Having recorded No 45120 at Dronfield, the photographer then travelled to Retford, where he captured this shot of one of the ageing 'Deltics' negotiating the cross-over on leaving the station, hauling the 1112 King's Cross-Scarborough service. I have to admit to a constant puzzlement as to how the drivers of these huge beasts could actually see out of their cabs, to safely guide their charges at high speeds. Indeed, even from this elevated view the driver of No 55008 *The Green Howards* can only just be glimpsed within! A rake of ballast wagons stands on the left, awaiting the engineer's call. *Brian Morrison*

▼ 15 September

Another DMU, another signal box and another level crossing: put the three together and they make another pleasing vista of a time on our railways now long gone. With the destination of Colne clearly displayed, Class 105 DMCL No M50788 heads into Huncoat station forming the 1635 service from Preston. The marks on the front end could be signs of age; indeed, having emerged from Craven's factory in October 1957, this unit was to have but three short months of life left, being withdrawn in December. However, scrapping – again at Mayer Newman of Snailwell – did not come until June 1984. Although now titled as a 'level crossing frame' and with only eight levers, the L&YR box dated from 1902, so at this date was approaching its 80th birthday. *Tom Heavyside*

▲ 17 September

The Peak Forest route, near Buxton, lost its passenger services on 1 July 1968 but, thanks largely to ICI and stone traffic, the line is still alive and kicking in the 21st century. Motive power and rolling-stock have changed greatly over the past 30 years, with some changes hot on the heels of what had gone before. Several classes of locomotive have disappeared from the scene for ever, such as No 25163, seen approaching Great Rocks Junction with an empty Northwich-Tunstead rake of ICI hoppers. *Tom Heavyside*

▼ 28 October

Once more, the careful use of framing – this time utilising station canopies and, on the left, the small electrical cabinet – turns what would otherwise be humdrum into a pleasing portrait. The 1140 service from Par has travelled the long and twisting single-track branch to arrive at Newquay's Platform 1. Once a thriving station, capable of handling long and not infrequent holiday specials intermingled with local services, the facilities are here reduced to just two platform faces; these were to be further reduced within 15 years, to leave just one outlet for passengers. The holiday season is over here, but the gentleman carrying the bulging suitcase is presumably here for a break, as he heads back into the rain, after temporarily enjoying the dry and comfort of Gloucester Class 119 DMU set P593. *Ray Ruffell*

1981

14 February

The destination blind on the DMU proudly states 'Special', and with good reason, for this train, seen stopped at Bury Bolton Street, was the last train to visit the Rawtenstall branch before final closure and handover to the preservationists of the emerging East Lancs Railway. Arriving from Manchester, via Castleton and the Heywood line, travellers on this train were enjoying the opportunity of the journey and the visit to the Bury Transport Museum; regular passenger services had been withdrawn between Bury and Rawtenstall nearly a decade previously, on 2 June 1972. *Tom Heavyside*

▲ 14 March

Another picture of a 'Rat' in revenue-earning duties, showing both the locomotive and train service in their latter years. Before the age of 'Sprinterisation' from the middle of the decade, longer-distance trains such as this Crewe-Cardiff service were formed of comfortable, largely Mk 1 stock, with plenty of space for passengers and the ability to see the passing countryside with ease. Seen at Caerleon, just a few miles out from Newport, the train, behind No 25042, seems to have been captured during a period of great excitement, judging by the number of photographers and their cars on and around the road bridge! Built as D5192 at BR Derby in April 1963 and initially working from Toton, TOPS renumbering came in February 1974. Withdrawal came on 8 May 1986, after which there was a trip to Vic Berry's yard in Leicester for cutting, completed by 31 October 1987. *Tom Heavyside*

► 20 March

What are not often or fully appreciated in these days of cosseted travel and/or mass production are the problems facing the railway builders and the more primitive tools, techniques and materials that were available to them. Yet they so often produced edifices and designs that were aesthetically satisfying and that have stood the test of time and increases in the traffic using them. Not least among these are the viaducts, and this magnificent example is at Calstock on the erstwhile Plymouth, Devonport & South Western Railway. Originally part of a light railway running from a junction with the Southern Railway at Bere Alston, this impressive structure carries the single line over the ever-widening River Tamar. Now part of the truncated Plymouth-Gunnislake route, DMU set L433 (comprising W51371 and W51433) crosses forming the 1325 service from Plymouth. *Tom Heavyside*

▲ 29 March

An alternative route between Scotland and Manchester, then as now, is the Settle-Carlisle line and thence through Blackburn. A more tortuous route – but a useful one in the event of problems on the WCML – there was no problem if the diagram was not an urgent one. One such is this train, a Glasgow-Manchester empty newspaper vans movement, seen leaving Bolton on the last short stretch of its journey behind No 40180. Some of the past importance of Bolton as a railway town can be judged from the infrastructure in view, with goods facilities both left and right of the passenger platforms. A product of English Electric's Vulcan Foundry in March 1962, as D380, and working from Camden depot in its early days, the Class 40 bowed out from Crewe Diesel Depot on 29 May 1983, to be 'reduced to razor blades' in the local Works complex within eight months. *Tom Heavyside*

▼ 16 April

On 17 March 1979 the former NBR Penmanshiel Tunnel was closed to all traffic, necessitating a diversionary route. Two years later another '40', No 40057, heads along this new route in the bright spring sunshine at the head of the 1707 Edinburgh-Newcastle express. Of earlier vintage than its 'sister' above, D257 started life in February 1960 at York sheds. Having acquired its TOPS number exactly 14 years later, it also outlived its younger sibling, surviving until withdrawal from Longsight on 23 July 1984. Cutting was also at Crewe Works, but this time not until November 1988. *Tom Heavyside*

▲ 20 April

As already remarked upon, there is no escaping the massive bulk of the 'Deltics'. Giving graphic illustration of the majesty and potential power of the class, No 55004 *Queen's Own Highlander* stands under Edinburgh Waverley's magnificent trainshed at the head of what will become the 1150 service to King's Cross. The combination of light and shade, the human and non-human detritus of a railway scene, and the carriages helping to lead the eye to the front-end focus of attention, all make for a very impressive and pleasing image. Though apparently an integral part of the scene, No 55004, introduced in May 1961 and named three years later, was to last but a few months more, being withdrawn on 1 November 1981. The oxy-acetylene torch had done its work at Doncaster Works by 23 July 1983. *Tom Heavyside*

▼ 20 April

The photographer is now at Millerhill Yard, a few miles south of Edinburgh, in time to capture No 40187 approaching from the west with a very mixed freight. While marshalling yards are still in use at various points in the 21st century, their number, style and extent have all changed dramatically over the last 20 years or so. In the glory days of humps, wide fans of tracks and constant train re-formations, before the widespread advent of block trains and company loads, they were home to many locomotives and their skilled operatives and were sights to behold. Sadly, so much of that has gone and the demise of Speedlink in 1991 sounded the death knell for many. Millerhill was to witness fluctuating fortunes during the 1980s and here looks to be mightily underused. *Tom Heavyside*

▼ 23 April

Another example of the old order on the ECML: the former Great Northern Tuxford station, between Retford and Newark, has long gone (together with the ex-GCR facility in the town) and the site is barely recognisable in this view of No 47405 powering its way south as the 1410 York-King's Cross express. The fifth of the 'Brush 4s' to be built, as D1504 at the company's factory in Loughborough, it emerged in January 1963 as Works No 346. In company with the first 33 of the class, its initial allocation was to Finsbury Park, on the southern stretch of the ECML, and it remained an ER servant for the whole of its life. During the last years before withdrawal, many of the first ten inherited celebrity status and nine were given names, '405' becoming *Northumbria* at Newcastle Central on 28 October 1982. Unfortunately, this did not ensure longevity; withdrawal came on 2 March 1986 and cutting, by a private contractor at Crewe Works, in December 1988. *Colin Marsden*

▼▼ 27 April

Another classic case of framing, and the end of the line in more ways than one. Once merely a stopping point on a G&SWR branch to Greenock (Albert Harbour), Kilmacolm became the terminus of the truncated stub from Johnstone, south-west of Glasgow, from 26 September 1966. 'Progress' is ongoing, however, and at the time of this view there were threats to close even this remaining stretch. Sadly, these were to prove real, the end coming on 3 January 1983. Here the 80mm lens gives a pleasing aspect to the still wintry birches and the creditably clean DMU waiting to return down the branch. The mixture of wood and stone is interesting in the station architecture, and efforts were made towards the end of the decade to re-instate the line. *Tom Noble*

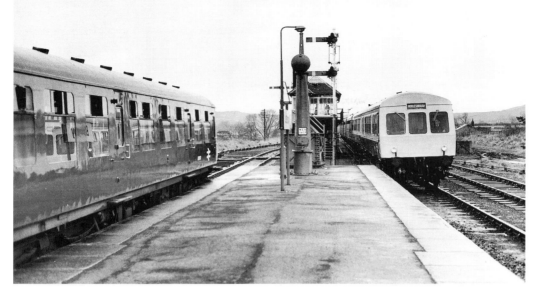

▲ 29 April

We have already seen one passing point on the Whitby-Middlesbrough line – here is another. This time the passing is achieved by means of an island platform, as opposed to the split layout seen at Glaisdale. With a coastbound service waiting for the road on the left, a return Middlesbrough-bound DMU, led by a Class 101 Driving Car and strengthened to five coaches, enters Battersby in distinctly indifferent weather. While a straightforward shot on its own, the semaphores, signal box and the proudly labelled 'NER 1907' water column all add to the scene. *Tom Heavyside*

▼ 30 April

Over the last 40 years or so marshalling yards were characterised by a hump to aid the sorting and collection of wagons, but there were many more throughout the country that fulfilled the main purpose of their larger brethren without such facilities. One such was York (North), which, as can be seen, occupied many acres and had separate fans of lines to handle traffic. In this view, looking south, the ECML curves sharply around the perimeter on the left as No 25027 eases its load of coal northwards, to eventually gain the main line. The dire effects of the miners' strike in the mid-1980s quickly put paid to many of the long-established pits throughout the country and, as a result, trains such as this. *Tom Heavyside*

▼ 2 May

The Glasgow-Edinburgh push-pull express service received much publicity during the 1980s, not least due to the culling of animals on the line (!), while changes to locomotive liveries and later operational practice received much less attention. In the long-reviled (but now fondly remembered!) 'Corporate Blue' livery, No 47710 *Sir Walter Scott* accelerates the 1030 eastbound service past Bishopbriggs oil terminal on the former NBR route out of Glasgow (Queen Street) station. First seeing life as D1939, the loco left Brush in April 1966 to serve on the London Midland West Coast Line (LMWL), and the TOPS scheme saw it become 47496 in March 1974. The 47710 guise was assumed in October 1979, when it became one of the 17 'Brush 4s' to be converted for push-pull for this cross-Scotland service, also receiving its name. Displaced from this duty by the decade's end, it moved south, in September 1990, becoming *Capital Radio's Help A London Child* at Old Oak Common on 17 August 1991. This name also went, in August 1993, to be followed by *Lady Godiva* in June 1994, and *Quasimodo* at Crewe in May 1996. Take your pick of the most suitable! *Tom Noble*

▼▼ 17 May

Once more, a slightly elevated vantage point and the inclusion of surrounding infrastructure all add to a pleasing result. With its clean lines aided by the uniform blue and grey of the Mk 1 coaches, No 46056 approaches the Stockton stop at the head of the 1713 Newcastle-Bristol service, diverted away from the ECML. The last 'Peak' to be built, D193 entered service on 26 January 1963 at Gateshead, became a '46' in November 1973 and remained an NE engine throughout. The type progressively became both unreliable and non-standard, accelerating the demise of the whole class by the end of the period under review. No 46056 succumbed, still at Gateshead, on 31 October 1982, from where it was despatched to Swindon Works for cutting by 9 November 1985. *Tom Heavyside*

► 5 June

Some 'nimbys' complain at having a railway close to their homes, but I doubt that many have the facility to park their cars this close to the tracks! The garden perimeter fences seem to be deteriorating or have disappeared completely in this shot of No 37067 leaving Dawdon Colliery, Seaham, Co Durham, with a rake of loaded coal hoppers. Once again, an observant photographic eye and careful composition have combined to forge a strong image, brought to perfection by the equally strong summer sunshine and the strategically placed wispy cloud! New in November 1962, its number here was lost on 13 January 1987 when it was one of a number reballasted to give a higher tractive effort, assuming the number 37703 in the process. Later developments saw it leave our shores to seek fame and fortune in Spain from May 2001, assisting in the building of a high-speed line there. *Tom Heavyside*

▼ 15 June

Week in, week out, the Cornish clayhoods went about their business receiving little in the way of widespread attention until their imminent demise. Suddenly appreciation was forthcoming, and hundreds of photographers descended on the county and points along the traffic's route to capture them before they disappeared for ever. This particular photographer, however, was aware of the situation and took the opportunities afforded to him by living in Devon to snap up images such as this – in bright early afternoon summer sun, No 47374 heads south through Totnes with a rake of empties. Though probably not as practical as their successors, especially when china clay dust poured forth, these older-style hoods certainly had an inherent charm. Once more, the careful awareness of composition, with the inclusion of the Creamery's chimney and the station buildings and footbridge, makes the picture that much more powerful. *Colin Marsden*

22 June

Framing, again, is important here, as well as the superbly controlled exposure. A shot from the other side of the barrier would have been nothing exceptional, but by including the opening and the detail in roof, canopy and posters, the photographer has contrived to present a satisfying image.

Seen at the Pwllheli terminus, Derby Class 108 DMU DMBS M50927 trails a four-car set waiting to return along the Cambrian coast to Machynlleth. Built in November 1959, this coach was withdrawn from active service in May 1992 and cut up at Gwent Demolition's site at Margam five months later. *Tom Heavyside*

22 June

An hour or so later, another four-car set from Pwllheli has commenced its journey as the 1030 service to Shrewsbury and has reached the trestle bridge at Penrhyndeudreath, with Derby Class 115 M51887 (in experimental livery) leading. At this time the route along the North Wales coast was threatened with possible closure, as the local County Council proposed to end the subsidy for travelling schoolchildren, the gunpowder works (in the background here) had recently closed, and Barmouth bridge had also been closed. Fortunately, the latter was re-opened and the line has seen a new lease of life, even to the extent of plans to trial the new ETRMS signalling concept along the route. Happily, M51887 survived withdrawal in February 1992 to reach safety in preservation. *Tom Heavyside*

▲ 22 June

Yet later on the same day, the focus has moved to the bridge at Barmouth, which was being 'eaten' by marine worms; BR's engineers were extremely concerned at the state of the largely wooden structure, its likely future, and the cost of any remedial work, especially as the latter was far from clear. The structure's precarious nature is well exemplified in this angle, as the 1240 Shrewsbury-Pwllheli DMU service sets out across the estuary waters, formed of a two-car Park Royal Class 103 DMU leading a Metro-Cammell two-car '101'. *Tom Heavyside*

▼ 29 June

Of all BR's freight traffic, perhaps that to suffer most during the 1980s was coal. As mentioned previously, the miners' strike did not help, nor did the economics of deep mining or cheap foreign imports. Over the period all the long-established South Wales mines closed, throwing many thousands of workers out of work and decimating the need for rail-borne coal shipments from the area. Sights such as this, at Maerdy Colliery, inexorably disappeared, leaving behind just the scars of what had been. No 37284 shunts a rake of loaded 16- and 20-ton wagons in the sidings, before heading off to its destination. In the distance an ex-BR Type 1 Class 14 'Teddybear' languishes in a siding, now belonging to the local NCB depot. *Tom Heavyside*

▲ 18 July

Another view of a coal train, this time a view of empties returning to the colliery. In yet another example of the clever use of the available infrastructure, including overhead gantries that at first sight might look to be ugly and intrusive, No 40184 approaches Stockport past the 'fortified' signal box. New as D384 from Vulcan Foundry in March 1962 and going straight to Camden shed, its TOPS number was used from February 1974. A largely uneventful life followed, with a wide range of work undertaken after removal from WCML front-line duties following the introduction of electrics, until withdrawal on 21 December 1982 and cutting at Doncaster Works one year later, on Christmas Eve 1983. *Tom Heavyside*

▼ 29 July

Viewed with the benefit of hindsight, the wedding of Prince Charles and Lady Diana Spencer was not the glorious occasion that it was hoped it would be. However, on the day there was much rejoicing in what can now be seen as much more naïve and forgiving times. After the wedding, the Royal couple took their first married steps towards their honeymoon aboard the train, seen here behind No 73142, appropriately named *Broadlands*, operating as the 1630 Waterloo-Romsey special and carrying the Prince's feathers as a headboard. The last of the English Electric electro-diesels built, in January 1967, and allocated to Stewart's Lane depot, the name was added at Romsey on 25 August 1980. Converted to No 73201 on 17 February 1988, to haul the 'Gatwick Express' non-stop shuttles, it was stripped of its glamorous name in 1999. *Colin Marsden*

▲ 11 August

Yet more careful framing: deliberately retaining the whole of the bridge arch and foliage to the right, which could have been omitted by another photographer, the DMU is then situated strongly on the 'golden third', heightening the effect of the train creeping stealthily into the station! Captured on his Nikon camera, using Ilford FP4 film, with an exposure of 1/500th at f5, the train is actually departing from Matlock, to run as the 0903 service to Derby. The rear coach is Swindon Class 120 DMBC No M50744, built in December 1958 and surviving until March 1987. The end came at Mayer Newman's site at Snailwell in January 1988. *Tom Heavyside*

▼ 24 August

Following the demise of steam and the initial interest in the former London Underground stock that took over the remaining stub of services, the railway on the Isle of Wight largely went about its business unheeded and unloved by the vast majority of railway enthusiasts. Even when there were rumours and threats of closure of the whole of the island's remaining track, there was little in the way of anguish on the mainland. Perhaps the weather in this view does not help, but the diminutive former tube stock does not inspire passion; unit No 044 arrives at Ryde St John's station in pouring rain, at the head of a Shanklin-Ryde Pier Head service. At least the semaphore and 1928-vintage, 40-lever signal box retain something of the old Southern flavour. *Tom Heavyside*

4 September

Apart from the volume and type of road traffic on the right and some of the buildings dimly seen in the background, this scene could have been from any period in the previous 20 years. From this familiar vantage point, portraying a train crossing the substantial and magnificent River Wear bridge linking Monkwearmouth and Sunderland, the coal traffic has not changed and even the EE Type 3 Class 37 and the concrete sleepers over which it is running were all around in the 1960s; even the drunken 20mph sign is at the same angle in views from that period! On this date in 1981, however, No 37242 is not as new and neither are the coal hoppers, which have remained unchanged over that period. Introduced to Worcester in September 1964 as D6942, it has survived into the 21st century, being sold into private hands towards the end of 2002. *Tom Heavyside*

▲ 12 September

To some, the Class 25s were 'Rats' – affectionately, of course – but to others they were underpowered and ineffectual, but by the time of their ultimate demise in March 1987 they, too, had acquired their own coterie of devotees. Happily, in this view, that time is still some way away. Two of a kind, Nos 25113 and 25139 double-head the 1007 Aberystwyth-Euston through train into Wellington. Salop. station. Though some rationalisation has been wrought here, with tracks lifted left and right, the whole scene still breathes life, with the station platforms and buildings clean, free of litter and well painted and the permanent way looking almost as good as it did in steam days, when lengthmen used to patrol their patch, keeping it clean and tidy. Freight, too, must still be a possibility, judging by the presence of the Class 08 shunter lurking in the bay platform. *Brian Morrison*

▲ 16 September

With all the play that was made with electrification at the end of the decade, on the ECML and with proposed schemes, it is often forgotten that some lines had been the beneficiaries of much earlier investment. Branches around the Wirral are a case in point, with ancient and ageing stock to prove it! Here a 1938-built Class 503 three-coach EMU, with M29273M leading, forms the 1221 Moorfields-New Brighton service approaching its destination. Looking attractive with its dated design, the class acquired an affection among its frequenters, especially towards the latter days before the withdrawal of the whole class, more or less en-bloc, at the end of 1984. *Brian Morrison*

17 September

A picture that captures all the elements to make a highly satisfying image: once more an elevated vantage point, sinuous curving track, the point of focus on the 'third', placing the subject in its context, and, not least, the human interest, helped here by their natural and casual attitude. Even the distant townscape is important, for the picture would have suffered if it had been cut off at the footbridge. Coming off the Southport sidings, No 40182 hauls the return daily freight for Wigan Springs Branch, portraying one aspect of railfreight that has all but totally disappeared, certainly since the demise of Speedlink in 1991 – the pick-up goods. The very concept became an anathema to rail authorities, but, thankfully, sense does seem to be returning in the 21st century, with the idea again being seriously considered and promoted. *Brian Morrison*

▲ 27 September

'Six days shalt thou labour and on the seventh rest.' Not so the railway! The architecture here is dramatic and fascinating and would no doubt send Lucinda Lambton into paroxysms of joy; it certainly provides a wonderful backdrop to the much less attractive and more prosaic cargo of waste wagons being delivered to Southall's sidings by No 47378. This is an empty GLC waste train, back from its run to Calvert dump with Londoners' discarded refuse – a 'nice little earner' for BR then, and for relevant companies since Privatisation, the Calvert site attracts similar tonnage from Bath and Bristol, and there are other such sites and workings throughout the country. *Tom Heavyside*

▶ 17 October

All too soon, it seemed, the last days of the 'Deltics' were upon us. All manner of specials and events were organised to recognise and celebrate the importance of the class and the work done by it over the previous two decades, and thousands of suddenly motivated enthusiasts toured the country to catch the last outings. Not surprisingly, well away from its normal stamping ground No 55015 *Tulyar* is very much the centre of attention as it pauses at Eastleigh station while hauling the 'Wessex Deltic' railtour. New to Finsbury Park from Vulcan Foundry on 12 October 1961 as D9015, the whole of its life was spent speeding up and down the ECML. Finally ousted by the influx of HSTs, official withdrawal was on 2 January 1982. Happily, preservation beckoned, and the unthinkable happened on 25 July 2003 when it was re-instated to official records and allowed to work the main line! *Colin Marsden*

1982

6 January

Twilight of the Gods! While the 'Deltics' had all the attention during 1981, finishing their work on the ECML, other endangered species were keeping their heads down, going about their business without fuss. On the Waterloo-Exeter route, the '50s' held sway, although not without an increasing preponderance of technical and mechanical problems.

Attractively caught in the lights of the late winter evening at Exeter (St David's) station, No 50011 *Centurion* pauses, having discharged its load, before proceeding to Plymouth (Laira) with the now empty stock. Note how the latitude of black and white film has successfully captured the detail in the ageing wooden awnings and the locomotive, while still maintaining interest in the brightly lit areas. *Colin Marsden*

► 10 January

Most of us tend to keep our hands in our pockets when bad weather strikes and put away our cameras; not so this professional and far-seeing photographer. Recognising the opportunities for different impressions in the winter snow, he has proved that it can give a surreal – and even glamorous – feel to the mundane, especially where the white stuff is whipped up into trailing clouds. Class 427 4VEG No 7907 leans into the curve on the approaches to Clapham Junction, operating as a Bognor Regis-Victoria commuter service. Note how the unit has obviously encountered snow en route, with the driver left with a less than clear window through which to observe the road ahead! *Brian Morrison*

▼ 23 February

As already stated, the Class 50s were the mainstay of the London-Devon passenger turns over the former Southern route, but in Cornwall they could and did put their efforts into a wider variety of work. In this view a low, weak sun gives an overall pleasing aura to No 50043 *Eagle* as it prepares to move out of Truro's goods yard with a distinctly ancient-looking rake of freight wagons, bound for Ponsandane, Penzance. Note also the equally vintage grounded box vans and wooden cabin to the left. In the foreground, No 37206 fills the void, waiting for its turn to work. *Brian Morrison*

▲ 27 March

Over the past 35 years, since the end of steam on BR, there have been mixed fortunes for the operation of that type of motive power on the main line. Swings in HQ opinion and support have led to occasional famines for the devotees of sights such as this, and into the 21st century the increasing stranglehold of the HSE has led to ever more draconian demands – and consequent escalation of costs – for steam operators. Locomotives have come and gone, as they reach the end of boiler certificates, etc, and it is now some years since the ex-S&D 2-8-0 had an outing. Here in LMS guise, No 13809 is most definitely the centre of attention as it heads the 'Cumbrian Mountain Pullman' past Arkholme, on the run from Carnforth to Hellifield. *Tom Heavyside*

▼ 10 April

As well as individual locomotive types being under threat at this time, so were a whole raft of DMU/EMU classes. One such is seen here, running into Guide Bridge station with a Manchester Piccadilly-Hadfield service. Having operated the line since their construction, and seemingly so permanent, the whole 506 Class was withdrawn en bloc in December 1984 and quickly despatched to Vic Berry's scrapyard in Leicester, from where they had all disappeared by the following May. Thankfully, three coaches were preserved at Bradford Transport Museum, but not M59602M shown here. Built at the confluence of the LNWR line to Huddersfield/Leeds and the GCR route to Sheffield, the size of the station complex is evidence of both the rivalry between the two companies and the amount of traffic handled in former times. *Tom Heavyside*

▲ 10 April

Later on the same day, a completely different vantage point is used to capture another of the '506s' going about its unsung business. Crossing the impressive Dinting Viaduct, which takes the railway across some marshy ground immediately on the approach to Dinting station, this three-car set is slowing for the next stop on a Manchester Piccadilly-Glossop/Hadfield service. The height of the structure can be judged from both the unit and the house on the extreme right. *Tom Heavyside*

▼ 17 April

Further north another example of a class shortly to be ravaged by withdrawals is seen in the form of Class 27 No 27107, heading north out of Aberdeen on the 0944 service to Inverness, past Kittybrewster on the old GNoSR route. Entering traffic as D5395 in June 1962, allocated to Cricklewood shed, it moved to Wellingborough depot on 30 November 1963, then operated on the Midland main line until migration to Scotland from 1968, in common with the rest of class. Renumbered to 27051 five months after this view, it was finally withdrawn, from Eastfield, on 6 July 1987. Another swift despatch to Vic Berry followed, and it had been cut up by the end of October. *Brian Morrison*

19 April

Many photographers eschew the opportunities of 'contre-jour' lighting, but, as shown here, the skilful use of such backlighting can bring an added 'sparkle' to an otherwise ordinary view. Here, the sun picks out the rails, the contours of the rock and the engine and carriage roof details to good effect, enhancing this view of No 47501 – then un-named, but to become *Craftsman* in 1987 – heading the 1135 Glasgow (Queen Street)-Aberdeen service past Hareness, south of its destination. It was to lose its name in 1997 and was withdrawn from squadron service on 12 July 2002, but this was not to be the end, for re-instatement followed on 6 September 2003.
Brian Morrison

▶ 25 April

We have already mentioned the decline in the fortunes of the 'Peaks', but here No 45076 is still in front-line service as it heads the cross-country 1555 Cardiff-Newcastle service across the viaduct outside Chepstow. Once again, the elevated view and the vertical format enhance the image, despite the even light from a dull day. Built at Crewe Works in December 1961 as D134 and allocated initially to Derby, it assumed its TOPS number in January 1975 and received a transfer to the ER. Withdrawal came from Tinsley depot on 12 November 1986, from where it was taken to March depot for storage. The eventual graveyard proved to be MC Metals in Glasgow, with the job finished by 11 March 1994. *Tom Heavyside*

▼ 26 April

The marriage of Lady Diana Spencer to Prince Charles moved her into the full range of Royal duties and benefits, and both are exemplified in this view of No 47511 *Thames*, departing from Exeter (St David's) en route from London to Bodmin Road for a private visit. Note the 'spit and polish' applied to the engine and the presence of the full Royal Train. This locomotive was to assume several different personae: D1955 (from new in December 1966 until March 1974), 47511 (until March 1985) and 47714, carrying the names *Thames* (as here) and *Grampian Region* (17 May 1985 to February 1989). Initially dispensed with at Crewe Diesel Depot on 21 August 1996, it, too, saw re-instatement, from 31 December 2001, as part of the burgeoning Cotswold Rail fleet. *Colin Marsden*

◄ 26 April

While Colin Marsden was snapping the Princess of Wales's train, this photographer was capturing this apparently much more prosaic sight of a DMU at Great Malvern station. However, there is interest here too, as this six-car set, forming the 1336 service from Birmingham (New Street), seems to be made up of three two-car units and one wonders why. The identity of the rest of the make-up is unknown, but the lead vehicle is interesting in its own right, being one of the then fast-diminishing Swindon Class 120s, latterly operating as Cardiff set C508. DMSL No 50666 was built at Swindon Works in May 1958 as No 53666, for cross-country work, but ended its days on less glamorous services. Withdrawn in April 1986, it was quickly scrapped at Vic Berry's yard in the same month! *Tom Heavyside*

◄ 27 April

The sheer size of Severn Tunnel Junction station and the area of land around it gives some idea of its past importance, and one wonders at the 'politics' and 'logic' involved in reducing the location, especially its once vital marshalling yard, to a virtual wasteland by the end of the decade – the acreage of railway land here that is now wasted is little short of criminal. As can be seen in this view, there was still life in the services at this juncture, albeit that seemingly only railwaymen have alighted as No 31414 restarts the 1301 Bristol-Cardiff stopper. In retrospect, six coaches does seem a little excessive for this short local service. *Tom Heavyside*

▲ 28 April

Once again the importance of a photographic eye and the clever use of local infrastructure to frame a picture is graphically displayed in this view of No 50033 *Glorious*, now in 'large body logo' livery, as it sweeps towards Exeter Central, nearing its destination with the 0910 Waterloo-Exeter (St David's) service. Many cried 'foul' in horror at the appearance of this livery, but 'time is a great healer' and in hindsight it does sit quite happily on the bulk of the '50'. New in July 1968, *Glorious* acquired its name at Laira on 26 June 1978, after transfer to the WR from WCML duties. Finally withdrawn on 25 March 1994, at Laira, preservation beckoned, with a transfer to the NRM at York within days. *Tom Heavyside*

▲ 29 April

It's never quite the same without semaphores! They add a distinct flavour to any railway picture, not least when they are out of the ordinary, as this stunted pair of up starters at Castle Cary. The twin-car DMU is also unusual, being a mix-and-match one-plus-one engineer's inspection train. Heading westwards, the two cars are now in Departmental service – Class 121 'Bubblecar' TDB No 975540 (ex-W55016) now adapted for route-learning purposes and KDW No 150266, then the Reading-based S&T Manager's GWR saloon but now preserved on the East Lancs Railway. *Tom Heavyside*

▼ 1 May

For reasons not appropriate for this space, 'Peak' No 45007 was my favourite and, being one of the last of class to be switched off, it is sad that it did not achieve preservation.

Here, with sleek, clean lines, it accelerates out of the curve at Aller Junction on the main line immediately south of Newton Abbot, at the head of the 0815 Birmingham (New Street)-Plymouth train. The signals on the branch to Torquay, approaching from the right, can be seen in the distance above the locomotive. New as D119, emerging from Crewe Works on 23 September 1961, it began work from Derby shed on 7 October. The next 20 years saw it on Midland main line expresses out of St Pancras, before being displaced by HSTs in 1982. Thereafter it gravitated to the ER, being graced with the unofficial name *Taliesin* at Tinsley depot in June 1987 (through the love of the Ffestiniog Railway by one official there!) before being withdrawn from that depot on 27 July 1988. Its final move was north to MC Metals in Glasgow, where it had been cut up by 6 November 1992. *Tom Heavyside*

6 May

These three views are from a visit made by the photographer to eastern Scotland. The first epitomises what the Comrie branch became – a lightly used industrial spur, little visited by either photographers or authority and largely left to nature to reclaim! On loan to the NCB, No 08719 is here slowly manoeuvring a rake of coal wagons along the branch, accompanied by an NCB employee. Once part of a Caledonian line linking Gleneagles with Balquhidder, the passenger services were withdrawn in two instalments – west to Balquhidder on 1 October 1951 and east to Gleneagles from 4 July 1964. In addition, the short westward stretch from Comrie to Crieff was also totally closed on the latter date, leaving only the eastern approach to Comrie; this, too, had gone by the end of the 1980s. Note the wonderful ex-Caley lattice signal post and fluted distant signal still in situ at this time.

Having run further down the branch with its load of coal, No 08719 now causes consternation for the road traffic at this unidentified crossing (*above*), with its delightful brick-based signal box. Built at Crewe Works on 31 May 1960 as D3887 and first seeing work at Edinburgh (Haymarket) shed, there were various transfers of depot within Scotland before it assumed the TOPS number 08719 in December 1973. By the time of its withdrawal on 22 November 1991 it had migrated a long way south, to Bletchley! It was disposed of at Gwent Demolition's site at Margam on 3 September 1994.

Back out on the 'main line', a coal train of a different sort is seen passing Cowdenbeath (*below*). No 20218 tails a very fully laden Thornton-Longannet MGR train being hauled by two further Class 20s. New from Vulcan Foundry on 25 November 1967 as D8318 and first sent to work at Haymarket shed, No 20218 also migrated south after its work dried up in Scotland, ending up at Toton, from where it was withdrawn on 4 October 1989. Its final journey was back to Scotland, however, for cutting at MC Metals in Glasgow, completed by 31 July 1991. *All Ray Ruffell*

1982

◄ 15 May

A chance conversation with Hugh Ramsey – then Editor of the recently launched *Railway Reflections* magazine – in which he commented that 'we would give our eye teeth to go back 20 years, to photograph what we thought would always be there', prompted me to point my camera at everything and anything. The value of this approach was proven only months later when, after seeing my wife on to a train to North Wales at Watford Junction station, I snapped this view of No 501108 at the suburban platforms on my way back to the car. The view has since been transformed, as the platform canopies and other infrastructure were all swept away to provide room for a redeveloped terminal section. The '501' EMUs were also to be short-lived, being progressively withdrawn from the middle of the decade and swept away from this site completely following the introduction of the newer '313' sets in 1986. *MJS*

▼ 28 May

Not inherently aesthetically stimulating, possibly, it is nevertheless interesting to compare the design and development of SR EMU front-ends. On the right, Class 405/2 4SUB set No 4356 is a Southern Railway design of four-car slam-door suburban units originally introduced in 1946 and built at Eastleigh between and 1951. By comparison, Class 423 4VEP No 7753 (left) was built by BR(SR) as express stock between 1967 and 1974. Seen in Clapham Cutting, the latter heads away from London with the 1050 Waterloo-Guildford service, racing past the former operating as the 1046 Waterloo-Wimbledon-Richmond-Waterloo circular service. *Brian Morrison*

▲ **29 May**

Oh happy day! At this distance in time, the sight of a 'Whistler' on front-line passenger duty under the wires on the WCML does your heart good! In glorious mid-morning sunshine on a Whitsun Bank Holiday Saturday, No 40126 draws to a stand at Lancaster station, taking enthusiasts, holidaymakers and day-trippers to the Cumbrian coast as the 0915 Liverpool-Barrow train. More prepare to join the train as it slows for the stop. Given life at English Electric's Vulcan Foundry on 21 December 1960 as D326, it immediately moved south to take up duties at Crewe North shed. Moving to various depots on the WCML over the next decade, TOPS numbering came in March 1974. Another ten years of service of various kinds then followed, before withdrawal from Carlisle (Kingmoor) on 15 February 1984; it was cut up on 21 April at Doncaster Works. *Tom Heavyside*

▼ **30 May**

The following day – Whit Sunday – at the other end of the country, the weather was not so brilliant, but this obviously did not stop crowds enjoying themselves, as can be seen by the multitude on the beach at Dawlish being typically British – determined to derive pleasure despite everything! Unnoticed by the vast majority on the beach and those buying Pollards ice-cream, a five-car DMU set headed by Class 118 unit B467 slows for the station stop as the 1535 Paignton-Exeter stopping service. One hopes that the man in shorts taking the photograph – bottom right – did not have his picture spoiled by the couple steadfastly marching towards him! *Ray Ruffell*

▲ 5 June

Another 'Whistler' is seen here on passenger duties. The '40s' were most definitely becoming the 'nation's favourite' as far as 'gricers' were concerned and many of these can be seen with heads out of the front two coaches as No 40184 leaves Chester with the 0900 York-Llandudno cross-country train. Though not in the foreground this time, the delightful and imaginative ex-LNWR gantry signal box provides an attractive framing for the background of the picture. At this stage, the former D384, new in March 1962, has just six months of service left, being withdrawn from Longsight depot on 21 December 1982. Like its 'sister' seen at Lancaster opposite, No 40184 was despatched at Doncaster Works, this time by Christmas Eve 1983. *Tom Heavyside*

▼ 5 June

Also at Chester on the same day, this view could have been taken straight out of a modelling magazine. Complete with stark rock cutting, greenery, clean trackwork and equally clean motive power, the view looks too good to be true. A mixed set of DMUs, led by Derby Class 108 DMCL No 52043, approaches the city with an unidentified eastbound service. When they first appeared – in No 52043's case, in 1960 – these 'railcars' were vilified by enthusiasts and railmen alike, ousting as they did steam from branch-line and other passenger duties, but with the advent of 'Sprinterisation' from the mid-1980s they suddenly acquired a status and affection that was both sudden and surprising. Withdrawn in August 1989, No 52043 met its end at Booth Roe Metals in Rotherham in March 1993. *Tom Heavyside*

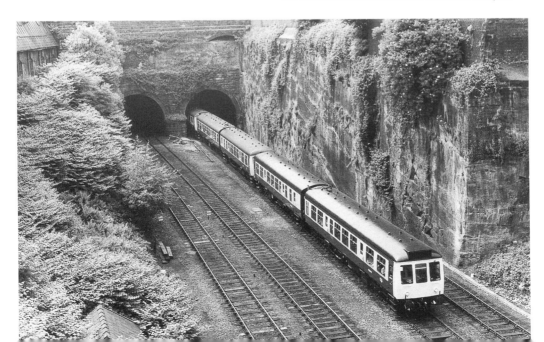

11 June

We have commented previously on the skill of this photographer in seeing, where mere mortals would just look, and here is another fine example. What small percentage of us, I wonder, would have chosen to use this view and vantage point that, on the face of it, 'loses' the DMU in the enormity of the station site? But by so placing it, balanced by the goods shed on the right and the snaking trackwork adding interest between, together with the appealing countryside beyond, we have a very pleasing and satisfying image. At first glance, Pontypool seems to have more than its fair share of land for a tiny rural station, but this belies its origins. At its heyday within the GWR, it served as a focal point for no fewer than six branches, and carriage sidings and other platforms would have been present and in use. That is all in the past, however, as Met-Cam Class 101 set B810 passes through with a down special train. *Brian Morrison*

▲ 16 June

In the early 1980s the railways in Scotland seemed largely overlooked and/or forgotten, but at the decade's close, not least through the magnificent efforts of Scotrail boss Chris Green, the country's railways became both revitalised and a Mecca for enthusiasts. Part of the reason was the sight of 'Growlers' – English Electric Type 3s – on passenger trains, a phenomenon increasingly absent south of the border. With rising mountains as a backdrop, No 37012, showing its pedigree with the split headcode boxes but proudly wearing the *Loch Rannoch* nameplate applied just two months earlier, accelerates away from Fort William with the 0834 Glasgow-Mallaig turn. 'Sister' No 37085 waits in the siding with a freight train, while to the left No 20191 receives some attention from a crew member. *Tom Heavyside*

▼ 19 June

Timing is everything, they say. The rain is pouring, but rather than put the camera away, I have strategically placed the car to face the tracks at Hemel Hempstead and used the windscreen wipers to clear a view. The trick was to co-ordinate camera shutter, train and wipers to capture the shot without evidence of wiper or smear on the image! Framed by the neighbouring car and sodden trolley and despite the poor light, the 1000th of a second shutter speed has successfully stopped No 86219 *Phoenix* as it roars into the station complex at the head of the 1550 Euston-Liverpool express. *MJS*

▲ 20 June

On the following day the storm clouds still hang ominously over the landscape as a 'Peak' in its last days on front-line Midland main line duties is captured just south of Syston, heading for Leicester. Despite its apparently timeless quality, much has changed at this scene, with a semaphore signal once standing by the quarter-mile post and a ballet-dance of telegraph wires once gracing the top of the poles; in addition, since this photograph was taken one of the slow lines (that nearest the camera) has been removed and the line slewed under the road bridge. No 45122 powers the 1200 Sheffield-St Pancras train along the easy gradients at this point, with a clear road ahead of it. *MJS*

▼ 20 June

Later that day, the view from the 'Birdcage', overlooking the site of Leicester shed, also evidences much that has both gone before and since. By the end of the decade, this view would have been impossible, screened by a growth of bushes, but had it been possible, the attractive ex-MR brick-built warehouse would have been missing, bulldozed in the name of progress. By that time, also, virtually all the motive power seen here would be in the great siding in the sky, with the light poles and far sidings all swept away. 'On shed' on this day are, left to right, Nos 45043 *The King's Own Border Regiment*, 47315, 08618 and 08695. *MJS*

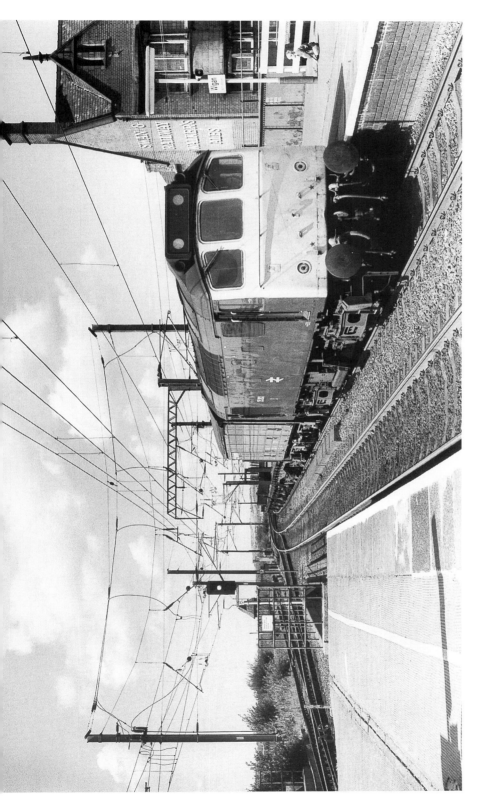

10 August

Here is a fine view of an immaculately clean 'Rat' under the wires at Wigan North Western in bright summer sunshine. No 25283 is heading south with an unidentified up freight, but what looks to be a short 'Speedlink' service. Built in October 1965, the loco's status as one the later examples of the class is betrayed by the clean front-end. Initially D7633, it first saw service at

41A Sheffield (Darnall) shed. Transfer to the MR came with a move to Wigan Spring's Branch depot on 14 October 1967, and it remained on the WCML route for the rest of its life. On 12 November 1985 it became No 25904, having had a life-extension 'E' exam and a top-speed reduction to 60mph; withdrawal did not finally come, from Carlisle (New Yard) depot, until 23 March 1987. Happily, it is still with us, preserved on the Severn Valley Railway. *Tom Heavyside*

1982

▲ 14 August

The blue and grey coach livery was standard for many years, but was overtaken from the mid-1980s by a change of corporate thinking regarding the business set-up and attendant liveries. It has now long gone, as has the 'Heart-Line' legend on the forehead of this HST. A Newcastle-Paignton cross-country service pauses at Rotherham for the waiting passengers to board. *Tom Heavyside*

▼ 14 August

Later that day, still in South Yorkshire, the photographer has successfully captured another 'Whistler' on passenger duties. This time on a cross-country turn, No 40034 reduces power and speed on the approach to Rotherham with a Cleethorpes-Manchester train, comprising nine coaches and three parcels vans. One of the early results of the Modernisation Plan of the mid-1950s, D234 entered traffic on 25 September 1959 at Crewe North shed. Assuming the name *Accra* in May 1962, it worked from various depots on the WCML before becoming No 40034 under the TOPS scheme in February 1974. The end of useful service came at Longsight on 8 January 1984, followed by a 'trip to the gallows' at Doncaster Works two months later. *Tom Heavyside*

▲ 14 August

This was obviously a good day to be around the Rotherham/Sheffield area for 'Whistler'-lovers! Having left Rotherham, the photographer has moved to Sheffield to see No 40029 passing Brightside with the empty stock from a Scarborough-Sheffield train. The inherent interest of the train is heightened by the framing of shapes and patterns made by the walls, bottom left, the colour light signal and the industrial complex on the right. The former D229 – named *Saxonia* in March 1963 – was withdrawn on 25 April 1984 and cut up at Doncaster Works the following December. *Tom Heavyside*

▼ 19 August

In many ways – not least due to a common constructor – the English Electric Type 3 resembled a younger brother of the '40' and, indeed, seen approaching head-on it was often difficult initially to tell the difference, apart from the slight 'cut-out' at the base of the bonnet on the '37s'. Unlike their larger kin, the '37s' had wide route availability and were seen at most points of the compass on our railway system. As if to emphasise the versatility of the work they could handle, No 37299 is here engaged on permanent way duties, heading a train at Goonbarrow Junction on the lonely Newquay branch. *Ray Ruffell*

▲ 21 August

Looking for all the world like some garden railway at a park, with the motive power slightly out of scale for the surrounding buildings, HST set No 253024 waits at Truro station to restart the journey northwards with the 1625 Penzance-Paddington express. In the early style of this livery, the 'barbed wire' logo and the 'cut-out' 'Inter-City 125' legend looked smart when kept clean, as on this power car. Note the ex-GWR lower-quadrant signal giving a clear road. *Ray Ruffell*

▼ 22 August

It is only in retrospect that the true magnitude of change can be assessed. Railway operations and infrastructure that once seemed so permanent often disappeared without fuss, but the change was no less dramatic for all that. At Loughborough, the warehouse that so dominates the scene is no more, the signal box has gone, Class 08s no longer spend time shunting here, and the ARC yard is unused, unkempt and with much track ripped up. Happily, the Midland origins of the station itself still remain and the Brush Works on the left still employs hundreds involved with railway construction and maintenance – and there is even talk of restoring the ex-GCR bridge over the Midland main line beyond the road bridge seen by the station. *MJS*

▶ 27 August

March was always a strange place – stuck in the middle of nowhere and yet a magnet for enthusiasts, drawn by the proliferation of freight workings and the ageing DMUs on local services. Like a vision of history, these two sets look smart, cared-for and purpose-built to offer the traveller a reasonable and safe journey. The station staff on the left watch as Cravens Class 105 DMBS No E51284 restarts the 1430 Cambridge-Lincoln stopper, while on the right a railman chats with the driver of '105' DTCL No E56468, before it regains the road as the 1240 Doncaster-Ely service. Exactly three months after this view the direct line to Spalding closed,

together with these two platforms! No 51284 retired in May 1987 to be cut up at Mayer Newman's in Snailwell the following October, and No 56468 went sooner, in October 1986, but succumbed to the cutter's torch at Snailwell later, in August 1988. *Tom Heavyside*

▼ 28 August

Over the years the cross-country Birmingham-East Anglia services saw a variety of motive power and fluctuations in fortunes. Nowadays space is limited on the two-or-three-car 'Sprinters', but in former times loco-hauled rakes of coaches would give the long-distance traveller more space and greater luxury. An example is seen here as No 31303 enters Cambridgeshire and Shippea Hill station, just a few miles short of Ely, with the 1414 Norwich-Birmingham diagram. The former D5836 of April 1962 later became 31458 on 4 December 1984, 31558 on 21 May 1990, and back to 31458 on 5 February 2001. Meanwhile, it had acquired the name *Nene Valley Railway*, at Orton Mere on 23 March 1994. *Tom Heavyside*

▲ 29 August

This is a delightfully rural scene, despite being in Greater London. Kent Coast express stock 4CEP No 411606 heads for the capital as a Ramsgate-Victoria service, about to pass a Maidstone semi-fast at Bickley Junction on the former SE&CR line to Bromley. The right-hand lines head for Petts Wood and Orpington. Ten years on, the left and middle pairs of tracks had been conjoined to give four tracks for the Bickley-Petts Wood chord. *Brian Morrison*

▼ August

Some of the character of suburbia is evidenced by the allotments at Chiswick as 2HAP No 6002 ambles on its unhurried way eastwards from Chiswick & Grove Park station, on the former LSWR route from Feltham to Barnes via Brentford, forming the 1228 Twickenham-Waterloo service. New in July 1957, the set was renumbered 5902 in May 1974, but regained its original identity exactly six years later, only to become one of the early casualties of the class, withdrawn in May 1984 and cut up in Leicester by Vic Berry the following January. *Brian Morrison*

30 August

As we saw on page 28, Kilmacolm station was under threat of closure and this actually happened in January 1983. There is, therefore, less than six months of life left in this view of No 101 340 waiting in the dull conditions to leave on a morning service to Glasgow Central, watched by the station staff and her dog! Carrying an 'AY' Ayr allocation sticker by the marker light, the unit was one of the type so often seen in and around Glasgow on services such as this and the Paisley Canal branch, and which in the 1990s acquired an orange and black livery from the Strathclyde PTE.
Ray Ruffell

1982

▲ **2 September**

We saw the Birmingham-East Anglia service on page 63 out in the countryside, but here one of the services is seen very much closer to one end of the trip, as No 31325 rounds the curve at Norwich Thorpe Junction with the 1015 service from Birmingham. Yet again the elevated vantage point adds interest to the view, together with the semaphores, squat signal box and background interest. No 31325 began life on 11 October 1962 as D5860, allocated to Darnall. Remaining an ER engine right through to renumbering to 31464 on 17 February 1985, it then spread its wings a little and finally ended up at Bescot, from where it was withdrawn on 4 January 1991. It was finally disposed of at MC Metals in Glasgow ten months later. *Tom Heavyside*

▼ **3 September**

Still in the Norfolk area, somewhat weaker (and stretched?) motive power is seen on the main line, as No 08250 approaches Trowse with coal empties returning from Norwich Victoria. The normal load would have been 4 or 5 wagons, and it is interesting to speculate why this abnormally long load should have been warranted. At this time, the '08' was one of BR's older locomotives, having appeared from Darlington Works on 16 October 1956, but appears to be taking the strain well! Originally No 13320, it became D3320 in February 1960 and 08250 in April 1974; throughout this time it was allocated to York. As might be guessed, by the time of this photograph its home was at Norwich, and withdrawal was from there on 30 November 1988. It, too, finished up at MC Metals, and was cut up by 7 August 1991. *Tom Heavyside*

16 September

In many ways the 'Peaks' mirrored the 'Deltics'. Both elbowed out previous regimes of crack steam express motive power to take over main-line duties, and both were in turn themselves elbowed out by HSTs. Perhaps not as spectacular as their larger brethren, the 'Peaks' were good, honest, reliable workhorses and many were sad to see them go. In the latter years of front-line Midland main line service, No 45 132 waits at Derby to restart a northbound train for Leeds, nicely framed by the signal gantry, although sadly without semaphores! The glancing early morning sun nicely picks out the clean lines. Subsequently finding work on cross-country and semi-fast passenger duties, as well as freight turns, No 45 132 ended its life at Tinsley on 10 May 1987, but happily there was life to come, in preservation on the Mid-Hants Railway at Alton. *Tom Heavyside*

1982

17 September

The early morning mist still hangs heavy in the background, partly shrouding the glory that is Newton Abbot station, but the sun has broken through sufficiently to pick out the detail of the magnificent signal gantry and the foreshortened Class 50 beneath it. No 50032 *Courageous* heads the 0758 Motorail train bound for St Austell. Judging by the number of cars loaded pathetically at the rear of the train, it is no wonder that the service was not long-lived. Gaining its name on 7 July 1978, after transfer to the WR, withdrawal beckoned on 15 October 1990, with the final cut being at Old Oak Common, courtesy of contractors Cooper's Metals, on 26 March 1991. *Colin Marsden*

▲ 20 September

A simple train, an uncluttered layout, but overall a pleasing picture: No 31282 is in no hurry as it ambles past Crag Hall signal box with a short rake of empties en route from Skinningrove to Tees Yard. Built in 1878 by the NER, the box was re-fitted in 1906 with 30-lever frame by McKenzie & Holland; it has no doubt seen much change over its life, and generations of its inhabitants could equally doubtlessly tell a tale or two! Built at Brush in September 1961 as D5813 and first allocated to Sheffield (Darnall) shed, No 31282 remained an ER loco until after TOPS renumbering in February 1974. Thereafter it moved westwards to the MR and ended its life at Crewe Diesel Depot on 7 January 1994. European Metals Recycling at Kingsbury finally broke it up on 6 August 2001. *Tom Heavyside*

▼ 21 September

Still in the North East the following day, attention has moved to Shildon, to record another scene that is no more. Between shunting duties at the ill-fated Shildon Works, Nos 08268 and 08063 stand temporarily idle in the autumn sunshine – with the gates to the Works complex firmly closed against them – apparently of no interest to the decorators of the local hostelry. At this time the two shunters had three and two years left respectively. *Tom Heavyside*

23 September

The apparent ordinariness of this image is deceptive, as there is so much of interest. Not least is one of the reasons for some retained use of the Settle-Carlisle route at this difficult time for the line – the MOD need for the Warcop branch, the remaining stub of the ex-NER branch that ran west-east from Clifton and the junction with the WCML to Darlington, via Kirkby Stephen. With a long consist of ammunition box wagons – the barrier wagon shielding the loco from potential danger! – No 40080, with just less than 12 months of service left, heads away from the branch at Keld, south of Appleby, with the moody magnificence of the surrounding countryside and the mountains in the background. The former D280 is a little over 20 years old here, but is on borrowed time. Having once been among the pride of the fleet at Gateshead shed when new in 1960, and spending much time on the ECML, the end came on the opposite side of the Pennines, at Longsight, on 11 September 1983. The final move, however, was back east again, to Doncaster, to finally disappear by 18 August 1984.

Tom Heavyside

▲ 15 October

And the winner is… The driver of No 25228, double-heading with another 'Rat', appears to be leaning from his cab, gloating at having beaten yet another of the class to the post! Captured at Castle Bromwich, on the western edge of Birmingham, it was unusual to see three of a kind like this at this late stage in their careers, especially as No 25228 looks to be coupled to an 'Ethel' (a Class 25 especially converted to provide Electric Train Heating – hence the acronym) and, therefore, a passenger working. The right-hand, unidentified, newer example is on a rake of coal hoppers. The former D7578 became 25228 in April 1974 and finally ended its days at Longsight on 20 March 1984, being cut up at Vic Berry's yard on 30 June 1987. *Ray Ruffell*

▼ 21 October

So many photographers fight shy of night shots, but, especially in black and white, there are so many benefits and there are images and effects that you just cannot obtain in daylight – and, in that medium, they are surprisingly easy! Black and white film tolerance is remarkable, with exposure latitude ranging over a couple of stops either under- or over-exposed. A sight no longer to be had and one that was becoming rarer even as this was snapped, is the sight of a Class 47 heading west from Swansea. On this night, No 47565 waits for a driver to take it out as the 2018 service to Milford Haven, with plenty of room for intending passengers in the four coaches in tow. *Tom Heavyside*

22 November

The lines out of Marylebone were under threat at the same time as the Settle-Carlisle route. There was to be a battle royal, and despite massaged traveller figures and grandiose schemes for guided buses using the trackbed – on top of a political antagonism to rail – the public won! Campaigners fought hard against dirty tricks and more 'lies, damned lies and statistics' and managed to mobilise support nationwide, even from quarters that had no need to use either the London terminus or the lines radiating from it. The poster on this platform seems to indicate that the struggle should not be so hard (!), but one wonders whether the two businessmen, casually strolling towards the concourse, had any idea of the strength of feeling in favour of their station. *MJS*

1983

7 February

Brrrrrr! It makes you feel cold just looking at this magnificent portrait of the now-infamous Ribblehead Viaduct. Typical Settle-Carlisle winter weather almost creates a white-out on Whernside in the background, as the photographer braves the cold and discomfort of the day to create this unusually angled view of a train about to sample the viaduct's windy exposure. 'Whistler' No 40152 gathers speed away from Ribblehead Quarry, carrying vital supplies of ballast to some far-off track relaying. Despite appearances, however, it is not destined for the north, as the locomotive will run round its train at Horton and return through Ribblehead in the up direction, to speed its train on to Healey Mills. *Brian Morrison*

◀ 9 February

This photographer must be a glutton for punishment, for, two days after the last view, he is still in the snow-covered fells! This time he has moved to the WCML to capture No 87013 *John O'Gaunt* at the head of the 0937 Carlisle-Euston InterCity express as it snakes its way through the landscape at Grayrigg. While I admit to a bias, it does not take a rocket scientist to see that rail is a much less wasteful user of land than road, a fact emphasised by the scar carved into the area by the M6 motorway, seen in the background. *Brian Morrison*

◀ 9 February

Moving south, the snows were obviously not as widespread at Lancaster! Another example of creative framing and good use of night photography – even to the extent of superbly capturing the building on the far side of the road bridge – makes a fine image of No 47455 at the head of the 1753 Workington-Huddersfield TPO duty. Within ten years the 'Brush 4' had been dispensed with and the TPOs followed by the early weeks of 2004, controversially scrapped by Royal Mail, supposedly to save money and improve postal services! *Brian Morrison*

▲ 26 March

A view just asking to be used as a 'past and present': in this view of No 31423 approaching Leicester (London Road) from the north, virtually everything of interest has since gone and the scene has changed dramatically. The traditionally Midland Leicester North signal box and the fantastic array of semaphores were all swept away with the closure of the 'Leicester Gap' later in the decade, whereby the last stretch of the Midland main line north and south of Leicester still covered by manual boxes was turned over to a new control centre. This was built on part of the site of the old engine shed, in the middle distance in this view, to the right of the train. The sidings at that point are no more and those to the left of this view have also disappeared. In addition, the Norwich-Birmingham cross-country service seen here no longer has the luxury of loco-hauled coaches, replaced by 2/3-car DMUs, while the 'Brush 2' heading this train, although still active in 2004, no longer undertakes this sort of duty. *Brian Morrison*

We previously saw the china clayhoods on page 31, with empties returning south to Cornwall. Here we see the loaded version, moving at a much slower speed with a far less powerful means of locomotion! Much of the business came from the Wenford Dries processing plant at Wenfordbridge, and here we see one trainload adding to the economics of both the industry and the isolated rural branch. In bright early spring sunshine No 08488 moves down the branch and approaches Dunmere

Wharf with a train prepared and ready for the main line and the run north. Initially built at far-away Horwich Works on 29 November 1958 as D3603 and allocated to Old Oak Common, it remained a WR engine for most of its life, finally being withdrawn from Cardiff Canton depot on 16 November 1986, having moved to South Wales after being replaced on the Cornish duties by Class 37s. Its furthest move north was to Glasgow, for a one-way ticket to MC Metals' scrapyard and the end on 21 April 1991. *Graham Roose, MJS collection*

▼ 1 April

The former North British Railway terminal station at Glasgow (Queen Street) was always cavernous, despite originally having a 'High Level' appendage, and viewed from today's vantage point it seems incredible that not only did it have full goods facilities, together with a 1 ton 10 cwt crane, but it also provided access for the transport of horseboxes and carriages/cars by rail. In recent times, the rail entrance to the station has been by way of a tunnel, achieved by building over the previous cutting seen here as No 37026 *Loch Awe* awaits the 'off' with the 1823 service to Oban. Note the 'Scottie Terrier' on the loco's bodyside, a telltale sign that it is allocated to nearby Eastfield depot. *Ray Ruffell*

▲ 2 April

We have now arrived at Oban and, after the mention opposite of Class 37s in Cornwall, this view shows the sheer flexibility and ubiquitous nature of the English Electric 3s. With the well-known landmark in the background, Nos 37026 *Loch Awe* and 37021 double-head the 1758 returning service to Glasgow Queen Street out of the town. Built in September and July 1961 respectively, both enjoyed varying identities. Though the latter remained anonymous throughout its career, the former carried the Scottish loch name from 6 October 1981 to 30 June 1986, whereafter it assumed an identity from further south – *Shap Fell* – between 6 September 1989 and 30 September 1996. They were both renumbered late in their careers, respectively to 37320 in 1986 and 37715 in 1988. *Ray Ruffell*

▼ 5 April

Still enjoying his brief holiday in Scotland, the photographer has now moved eastwards to Perth, where he has been fortunate in the positioning of these engines, to provide a pleasing head-on view enhanced by the diagonals of the buildings right and left. Nos 26029, 26040 and 27024 stand temporarily switched off between duties in the sidings to the west of the main station complex. Although all built by the Birmingham Railway Carriage & Wagon Company and initially consecutively numbered, what became the '26s' and '27s' were separated by two years in build and ended up differentiated within TOPS. New in June and September 1959 and January 1962 respectively, the two '26s' began life at Haymarket shed, while No 27024 cut its teeth at the then fairly new Thornaby Diesel Depot. *Ray Ruffell*

▲ 9 April

We looked earlier at the benefits of 'standing back' and putting the train in its context. Here is another example of that ploy at work, made all the more successful than a straight front-three-quarter view by virtue of the inclusion of the shallow embankment, angle of light, attractive cloud formation, and the farm and Stokesay Castle in the background. In the days when such sights were a common feature of our railway landscape, No 47257 heads north with a Bristol-Manchester parcels train. *Tom Heavyside*

▼ 11 April

Once again the inclusion of surrounding infrastructure helps make the picture far more than a close focus on the train. With, to the left, the squat Furness-style signal box, built around 1874 and re-fitted in 1977 with a second-hand LMR standard frame of 14 levers, and one of the semaphores under its control signalling the departure of another train, a six-car DMU, led by a Class 108 twin, enters Bootle as the 1420 Carlisle-Preston service. It is an unusually long rake on the face of it, and a strange place to capture a service that should terminate further north, but this was the standard formation for this train, as it carried a capacity load of workers from BNFL at Sellafield to various stations south! *Ray Ruffell*

▼ 22 April

For some reason I never visited Broad Street station in steam days, although it was literally next door to Liverpool Street, which I did visit, and I only came to know the former and develop an affection for it in its terminal years, so to speak. Compared to the constant hustle and bustle of both Liverpool Street station and the area of London around it, Broad Street was a haven of peace and tranquillity, like stepping into a period piece. By this time, only the more westerly platforms were in use, with those closer to Liverpool Street station being heavily overgrown and access to the platforms only by way of the side stairs, with the main entrance permanently closed. Still in all-blue 'Corporate' livery, EMU set No 501178 (with coach 75178 leading) waits to form the 1641 service to Watford. Note the massive reduction in protection from the weather caused by the removal of much of the trainshed. *MJS*

▶ 22 April

On the same day, next door at Liverpool Street, Class 37s still took the lion's share of the East Anglian passenger work out of the station. Gently idling at the head of its stock, as the crew approach from the dark recesses of the station, No 37050 will soon depart with the 1650 to Ipswich. Displaying its early parentage, with the twin headcode boxes and front gangway doors, life began for D6750 on 24 August 1962 at Sheffield (Darnall) shed. Moving to East Anglia (at Ipswich) exactly five years later, its pre- and post-TOPS life was spent operating over the region and into London. In January 1989 it was reballasted to increase its tractive effort and re-numbered 37717. This took it further afield and it has received and lost many names; becoming first *Stainless Pioneer* on 1 August 1992 at Thornaby depot, it subsequently acquired fame as the locomotive chosen to bear many of the annual junior

school 'Railsafe Trophy' winners' names – *Maltby Lilly Hall Junior School Rotherham* in 1996, *St Margaret's Church of England Primary, City of Durham* in 1997 and *Berwick Middle School* in 1998! *MJS*

22 April

Despite all the electrification and the onset of units supplanting loco-hauled trains, there was still a need for the occasional shunting duty and a station pilot at Liverpool Street. Whereas in steam days the duty would have been carried out by an immaculately turned-out engine, those days were a fading memory by this time and No 08531, seen in the first picture with two largely empty wagons, is in no special condition other than 'work-weary'! Emerging from Darlington Works on 1 April 1959 as D3693, initially to Hornsey, it remained an 'Eastern' engine throughout and was still active in 2004.

Evidence of the 'unitisation' referred to above is seen here with a Class 315 unit entering the station with near-empty stock, ready to leave some time later with a throng of homeward-bound commuters. Though small in the picture, the framing from inside the overhead covers, the spotters on the left and the juxtaposition of light and shade all add to the overall finish.

The day has now 'turned nasty', with driving rain streaking the train's roof as commuters have scurried for cover from the eight-car Class 115 1742 Marylebone- Aylesbury service at Amersham, and the guard peers from his position on the last carriage, waiting to give the 'all clear'. By the end of the decade these first-generation 'Heritage' DMUs were being replaced in great numbers, but the route to Aylesbury was fairly late in receiving the new stock. *All MJS*

▲ 23 April

The following day, further north, the weather has improved dramatically. Still hanging on to front-line duties, 'Peak' No 45131 waits at Sheffield Midland to become the 1235 express service to St Pancras, while on the right a Swindon-built cross-country DMU set is gathering custom for the SLS/BLS 'Wyvern Express' tour. *Ray Ruffell*

▼ 26 April

With the garden bushes and trees on the railway's boundary beginning to show new leaf, another 'Peak' demonstrates the variety of work that the class increasingly fulfilled in its latter years. Looking at home in the bright spring sunshine, No 45063 approaches Taunton from the south with an up parcels duty. Emerging from Crewe Works on 1 June 1961, the erstwhile D104 went new to 17A Derby. Thereafter it remained a Midland main line engine for the whole of its life, although travelling to disparate parts of the UK, until final switch-off on 5 May 1986. It was yet another victim of Vic Berry's yard, vanishing by 9 August 1988. Note the attractive skew bridge in the background and the presence of the ex-GWR water tower. *Tom Heavyside*

28 April

An 'ordinary' train is successfully captured on film, in an image obeying all the rules: the use of the low light, elevated angle, curving train and tracks, inclusion of signals and the counter-balancing of road and large building on the left with the warehouse on the right. No 50009 *Conqueror* swings north around the final curve before Truro station, slowing to pick up more passengers for the 1815 Penzance-Bristol service. Even ignoring the duo of parcels vans attached to the rear, note how luxurious is the accommodation compared to what would be served up in the 21st century! *Tom Heavyside*

▲ 29 April

Still in Cornwall on the following day, the photographer has alighted at Bodmin Road and stepped towards the old Bodmin General branch to witness No 37207, carrying the locally appropriate *William Cookworthy* name, leading the Chipman weedkilling train as it retraces its steps from Boscarne Junction. Later into the decade, much was made of these trains being topped-and-tailed by specially converted Class 20s. *Tom Heavyside*

▼ 29 April

Swinging round nearly 180 degrees, the station nameboard announces the bus connection for Bodmin, Wadebridge and Padstow as, still in 'small blue' livery, No 50047 *Swiftsure* enters the station with a relief Paddington-Penzance service. Note the attractive ex-GWR footbridge and the substantial platform signal box, now converted to a café. *Tom Heavyside*

30 April

From their introduction in the 1960s, the WCML electrics, especially the Class 86s, have stormed back and forth up and down the western flank of the country transporting many hundreds of thousands of passengers. Even through the evolving Sectorisation and Privatisation periods, when coats of many colours were de rigueur, they seemingly went about their business unheralded, so the previous all-blue era could have made them virtually invisible! Beneath an ominous leaden sky, No 86230 *Duke of Wellington* roars through Watford Junction station, non-stop, at the head of the 0740 Manchester-Piccadilly-Euston express.

On the same day, at the other end of the route from Broad Street, a Class 501 unit stands ready for the fray at Watford Junction, but bound for a different destination. Standing at the suburban platforms, which were within weeks of destruction, and showing the structures and buildings that were destroyed, No 501153 waits to leave as the 1025 2nd Class-only stopper to Euston. The driver approaches, cup of tea at the ready, but apparently of no interest to a young Tammy Stretton!

Gerrard's Cross station, also seen on 30 April, has seen changes to its layout and thoughts about its future in the past 20 years or so. In this view the site still retains its central through lines, a legacy of the GWR and the Paddington-Birkenhead expresses. However, these tracks were ripped up shortly after this view and, into the 21st century, the aspect has undergone even more amendment, with the nearest (up) track being removed, the up through being replaced and the platform built out to meet it. This view is now impossible, however, due to the growth of trees over the ensuing period. *All MJS*

▲ 7 May

Over recent years the trackwork around Wakefield has seen
much rationalisation and downgrading, not all of it, it has to
be said, either advisable or successful. One location to suffer a
reversal of fortune and traffic and drastic indignity during the
1980s was Goose Hill Junction, Normanton. Somewhat
incredibly, it was the former Midland Railway main line from
Sheffield/Rotherham to Leeds that was sacrificed (seen here
as the left-hand route), with the former L&YR 'deviation'
route via Barnsley surviving. Seen before this desecration, No
31324 comes off the L&Y line and heads past the attractive
signal box and semaphore gantry – both now gone – with an
engineer's train. *Tom Heavyside*

▼ 14 June

If they did nothing else, the Victorians crafted and bequeathed
to us some magnificent structures, be they tunnels, trainsheds
or viaducts. Though not as famous as some others, Cynghordy
Viaduct on the 'Heart of Wales' line has a distinct charm, with
its uniform and attractively lined arches, here dwarfing the
twin-car Metro-Cammell DMU running through the
spectacular scenery forming the 1050 Shrewsbury-Swansea
service. *Tom Heavyside*

1983

15 June

Having travelled down the 'Heart of Wales' line, the photographer has now reached Pontyates on the ex-Burry Port & Gwendraeth Valley Railway in Carmarthenshire. Gauging dimensions on the branch were such that standard BR locos could not work it without being trimmed. Cwm Mawr Colliery was the reason the route survived into the 1980s, and on this day Nos 03145 and 03141 display their cut-down cabs as they pass the old station with empties for the colliery. They survived until July 1985 when they were sold, as going concerns, to White Wagtail Ltd in Coventry. *Tom Heavyside*

▲ 16 June

Now a selection of views from Swindon Works in its final years. To witness the decline and eventual closure of the once proud Works during the early to middle years of the 1980s was one of the saddest events of the decade. The institution, with the famous and much-missed 'A' Shop, boasted a loyal, proud and tremendously skilful workforce and the feeling of abandonment in the town with the closure was palpable and did the railway industry great harm locally and nationwide. Discarding it as a wasted asset was no way to win friends! The writing was on the wall when a group of bankers paid a private visit on this day. Some can be seen on the right, walking away from No 37167 as it awaits attention, minus one buffer. *MJS*

▼ 16 June

An unusual sight inside 'A' Shop on that day was December 1960-vintage 'Whistler' No 40127. Already withdrawn – from Wigan Spring's Branch 16 months earlier – it waits to be cannibalised for spares rather than enjoy a happy rebirth. The demolition had been completed by 13 August. *MJS*

◀ **16 June**

Another view inside 'A' Shop provides an interesting comparison with well-thumbed illustrations in books and magazines showing GWR steam locomotives in these rows for attention; this day could only provide 'Gronks'. Nearest the camera is No 08795 – D3963 of 21 May 1960 from Derby Works – while 'sister' No 08778 – D3946, also from Derby, on 2 April 1960 – is without its innards a couple of rows down. A WR engine for the whole of its existence, No 08795 was still alive in 2004, working from Landore depot, whilst

'778 was originally an incumbent of York, then the ER, before moving some time later to Cardiff (Canton) from where it was withdrawn on 25 September 1992.

While the '08s' were receiving attention inside, there were lines of withdrawn and abandoned locomotives outside. With 'A' Shop in the background, No 08281 (right) is wedged in by wagons, unlike its 'sisters' on the left, including 08125, 08574, 08303, 08559, 08265 and 08178. Many quickly disappeared, but, incredibly, '303 and '265 escaped and survived until 1987! *Both MJS*

▲ **30 June**

Children of the 1955 Modernisation Plan, the 'Choppers' – Class 20s – obviously had steam ancestry, with their cab at one end facing a 'boiler'. From early years they were 'tandemed', to both help with tractive effort and to improve visibility when working 'tender first'. Although pairings were not permanent, solo workings became very much the

exception, especially as loads increased. Midlands coal traffic for power stations, from a base at Toton, was one of the Class's staple diets and one such working is seen here, as Nos 20208 – one of the few with mini-snowploughs - and 20032 double-head a rake of very full wagons past Clay Cross. At this time No 20208 was a recent transfer south from Scotland, hence the presence of the snowploughs. *Brian Morrison*

▲ 1 July

A little short of ten years after this view, early in 1992, it was announced that the line from Leicester to Burton-on-Trent (named 'The Ivanhoe Line' in true marketing-speak) was to be re-opened for passenger traffic. Just how much attention would need to be given to the trackwork in the area around Moira West – and indeed other stretches of the route – can be seen in this view of No 56051 negotiating a road severely affected by mining subsidence, as it hauls an empty MGR train from Drakelow Power Station. *Colin Marsden*

▼ 6 July

Although renovated at Brush Works in Loughborough midway through their careers, the Class 46s were still non-standard and thus an anathema to BR in the 1980s. Their early demise was thus assured. Here, No 46026 *Leicestershire & Derbyshire Yeomanry*, still proudly wearing its nameplates, outwardly looks in fine fettle as it smoothly hauls a southbound HTV train past York, Dringhouses, yard. The sole member of the class to be named, it was withdrawn from Gateshead depot on 25 November 1984. Once more notice how sparse is the traffic in the spacious goods yard. *Colin Marsden*

▼ 14 July

Not only did locomotives receive new coats during the decade, so did rolling-stock. Ironically, looking from the vantage point of events early in 2004, Royal Mail stock was not exempt from this, and a whole new image was created in the 1990s, moving away from the two-tone look seen here.

With the station lamps shining like fairy lights around and reflecting off the train, No 45140 once more shows off its clean lines within the confines of Exeter (St David's) station, at the head the 1922 Penzance-Paddington TPO. It will come off at Bristol, perhaps to be replaced by a Class 47. *Colin Marsden*

▶ 17 July

One development that was kept very quiet from the average enthusiast until after the event was the refurbishment and repaint of the original 'Whistler', D200. Built as the pioneer Type 4 express passenger type and entering service on 14 March 1958, it ushered in a new generation of motive power on the East Anglian route out of Liverpool Street. Feted as the class and type leader, its fame was somewhat diluted when it was renumbered 40122 under TOPS in April 1974. It was withdrawn without ceremony on 23 August 1981, and, to the disbelief of many, the NRM in York saw no reason to save it for the National Collection, despite its historical relevance! Happily, it was officially reinstated on 25 April 1983 and is seen here inside Toton depot receiving that repaint. The overalls belong to the depot foreman and he was none too pleased at the sound of my camera shutter, not wishing his secret to be out too soon! *MJS*

18 July
Another view of what was left of the once-superb trainshed at Broad Street, with what seems to be a rather inappropriate advert for the time and location – 'Inter-City makes the going easy'! Unit No 501151, with M75151 leading, is already 10 minutes late, according to the clock, as it is scheduled to leave at 1135 with a service to Richmond. With a carriage door open and the guard seemingly unhurried, perhaps the timepiece is at fault…? *Brian Morrison*

▲ 18 July

On the same day as Brian Morrison was at Broad Street, this photographer was at the other end of the country. At Achnasheen, a passing place on the long Kyle of Lochalsh-Dingwall single-line branch, No 26052 stands as light engine, waiting for No 37260 to pass with a rake of empty low-sided wagons. The guard at the rear of the locomotive leans out of his cab to exchange single-line tokens, allowing access to the next stretch of the route. Elsewhere, a motley crew of rail staff and general public wait for a passenger service; from the expression on some of the faces, they are wishing that this train could whisk them away! *Tom Heavyside*

▼ 19 July

The following day the photographer has reached one of Michael Palin's favourite stations. In the days when there was still some variety in Scottish services, especially through the Highlands, No 26032 stands in the single platform at Kyle of Lochalsh, waiting for passengers from the Skye ferry, to eventually go forward as the 1110 service to Inverness. Judging by the look of the weather across the water, those passengers may well be pleased to head east! *Tom Heavyside*

1983

▲ 21 July

On this day John Slater, then Editor of *The Railway Magazine*, was giving a talk to a group of local railway enthusiasts. While waiting to meet him at the station, I took the opportunity of capturing this view of the much-reduced facilities at Marlow, at the end of the 1839 branch from Maidenhead. A shadow of its former self, it is fortunate that the weather was so good as there is no waiting shelter for the seated young lady also awaiting the train. London-based DMU set L284 draws to a halt, with commuters already opening the doors to make their escape. *MJS*

▼ 30 July

Yet another 'Peak' eking out its existence on passenger duties: approaching Moorthorpe, on the old Swinton & Knottingley Joint Railway route between Pontefract and Swinton, No 45149 heads the nine-coach 1404 (SO) Scarborough-Luton service. Once more the elevated angle gives an added dimension, with the splitting of the line to the left – to Wakefield – balancing the houses on the right, and the brightly lit train perfectly positioned within the frame, all adding to a very pleasing portrait. *Tom Heavyside*

1983

3 August

By the seaside – but not Dawlish or Blackpool! – a handful of intrepid holidaymakers seem determined to enjoy the delights of the Thames Estuary at Leigh-on-Sea, complete with chair, transistor radio and Lilo, blissfully unaware of the train behind them, or that it is your author's 40th birthday! Judging by the beached vessel *Bembridge*, these fun-lovers will have to move when the tide comes in! Two ER Class 302 EMU sets, with No 302302 leading, seem to be in a hurry to pass the water's edge as they form the 1512 Fenchurch Street-Shoeburyness service. Note the yachts, all high and dry and covered up. *Brian Morrison*

1983

▲ 6 August

Just one more example of the creative positioning of the train within its landscape and context. With a delightful setting of the sort of railway architecture that was once taken so much for granted – with the exception of the unusual overhead signal cabin – HST power car No 43087 heads over the Selby Swing Bridge with the 1755 York-King's Cross express service. Sadly, like the abandoned signal box, the line was to see its importance stripped from it, with ECML trains being diverted. *Tom Heavyside*

▼ 14 August

Here is another view of the electrification system that Merseysiders had known for many years and which preceded the proliferation that has come in more recent times. Still displaying great style, not least because of the tastefully conceived 1938 design, although beginning to look just a little dated – despite the disguise of standard 'Corporate' blue and grey livery – Class 503 MBS No M28392M stands in Birkenhead Central station ready to take its train to Rock Ferry. Like so much other stock seen in this volume, this coach was cut at Vic Berry's site, in September 1985, having been withdrawn just six months earlier. *Tom Heavyside*

▲ 29 August

One of the features of the 1980s, after the sudden reversal of fortune at Marylebone, was the resurrection of steam on the main line, to the delight of enthusiasts and the general public alike. One of the early regular runs was a round-trip excursion from York to Scarborough as the 'Scarborough Spa Express'. On this day, standing under York's magnificent arched trainshed roof, superbly restored 1937-vintage Stanier 'Black Five' No 5305 – sometime based at the Keighley & Worth Valley Railway – waits for the road. Sadly, the engine failed just 5 miles out of the city and had to be rescued by fellow steam favourite *Evening Star*! *MJS*

▼ 29 August

Later in the day HST power car No 43113 hides in bay platform 10 at York as empty stock; this was the first HST car to be named – *City of Newcastle upon Tyne* at Newcastle Central station on 26 April 1983. Losing the name on 28 February 1989, it regained it on exactly the same date four years later, to be shorn once more on 30 April 1997. A further naming followed in December 2003, when it became *The Highlands. MJS*

▲ 1 September

Imposing London office blocks tower above the streets and dominate this view, contrasting starkly with a previous generation of architecture on the left, while there are also contrasting styles of SR rolling-stock. Slim-bodied Hastings Line unit No 1002 (left) forms the 1245 Charing Cross-Hastings service trying to race later-designed Class 415/1 4EPB No 5140 forming the 1244 Charing Cross-Orpington train towards Waterloo East. *Brian Morrison*

▼ 7 September

As we have already seen, the Cornish clayhoods were becoming a well-loved institution, and were a definite link with a past era; while the replacement stock certainly reduced the escape of clouds of clay dust en route, they did not have the charisma of these 'tents'. In those more picturesque times, No 47205 heads a down special of empties, approaching the Exeter Bypass at 1135 on a bright late-summer morning. *Colin Marsden*

7 September

There cannot be many enthusiasts who do not know Dawlish and its seafront – either personally or through countless images in railway publications. However, the same probably could not be said for Class 33s operating along the wall. Later the same day, No 33058 is here employed to replace a shortage of ageing DMU stock prior to the ill-fated introduction of 'Pacers', forming the 1425 Exeter-Paignton local service on the approach to Teignmouth. *Colin Marsden*

▲ 1 October

At Edinburgh Waverley station, this time at night, we see another example of the wider view emphasising the time of day and the isolation of the train with a complete absence of passengers visible. The picture has a cold, early-hours feel about it as No 26026 stands at the head of empty stock, ready for when the call comes to wake up and perform the required duty. Built by BRCW as D5326 in May 1959 and allocated to Haymarket, it remained a Scottish engine through until withdrawal from Inverness on 24 November 1992. Final disposal was also in that country, at MC Metals in Glasgow, by 22 June 1995. *Tom Heavyside*

▼ 13 October

Another example of framing, including some human interest, and not putting the camera away in the pouring rain. On a particularly dull, damp and dismal day at Oxford, No 50039 *Implacable* draws into the station with the 0950 train from Paddington. The indicator board announces that the train terminates here – no doubt the driver of the 'Hoover' is relieved! *Implacable* ended its career at Old Oak Common on 4 June 1989 and had been cut up there by 6 July 1991. *MJS*

22 October

There are not many places in the UK where trains are allowed to be quite this close to cars – usually, the two are kept very much apart! Even with a railway employee walking in front of the train, it was not always plain sailing – if you will excuse the pun, next to the harbour – as not all motorists were assiduous in keeping to their designated parking spaces! Here No 33112 slowly threads it way through the decidedly cramped route at Weymouth Quay with the 0935 train from Waterloo approaching its final destination. This view graphically displays the potential problems and explains why the facility was constantly under attack from authorities. By the end of the decade the route was disused, meaning that travellers to and from the Channel Islands and Cherbourg could no longer enjoy the luxury of being taken by train right to the ferries' 'doorstep'. *Brian Morrison*

▲ 3 November

Two more Class 33s, in duplicate this time to effectively handle the long and heavy train behind them. On a dull and misty late-autumn morning, Nos 33106 and 33006 grind their way past Halling, on the Strood-Maidstone branch, with the 1000 Allington-Westbury train of empty hoppers. Both built within four months of each other in 1960, the two 'Cromptons' saw their 30th birthdays, but succumbed to age, changing traffic patterns and the influx of new motive power to be withdrawn on 16 November 1990 and 6 August 1991 respectively. *Ray Ruffell*

▼ 12 December

More double-heading, this time by the more powerful Class 56s, on another long and heavy load. In bright winter light Nos 56032 *Sir De Morgannwg/County of South Glamorgan* – with one of the larger nameplates! – heads an unidentified 'sister' along the GWR main line near Pengam Junction with a Port Talbot-Llanwern ore train. *Ray Ruffell*

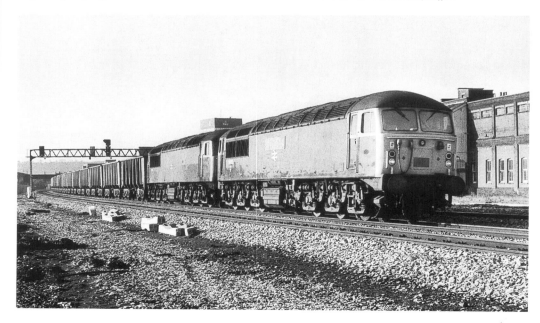

17 December

A truly delightful picture with which to round off the year. As seen before, a number of locomotives were restored to main-line condition and put to work on special charters in the early 1980s. One such glamorous and historically important example is seen here entering Hellifield station, beautifully framed by the magnificent ex-MR tracery and canopy that is just about keeping the photographer clear of the damp conditions outside. No 46229 *Duchess of Hamilton*, built in 1938 and once streamlined in red and gold – and, in the early war years, touring the USA as No 46220 *Coronation* – passes the 1911 MR South Junction signal box with a 'Cumbrian Mountain Express' from Leeds to Carlisle. Note the still extant semaphores and the miserable-looking souls on the distant platform. *Tom Heavyside, John Keylock collection*

103

1984

13 March

As well as steam charters, mainly for the enthusiasts, there have been numerous others, of different motive power and for alternative clientele. About to pass the 60-lever former LMS box at Bootle, built in 1933, No 33113 provides some colour to both its surroundings and the dull day while hauling a rake of 'Gatwick Express' stock around the North conveying holiday company reps. Starting its journey as the 1530 from Manchester, the train is here on its way to Chester, where it will be stabled overnight. *Colin Marsden*

▲ 15 March

Two days later the touring duties of the train seen opposite are over and the locomotive and stock are bound for home territory south of the Thames. Still in very dull weather conditions, No 33113 is again seen with its glamorous exhibition train stock passing Rotherham on the way south as the 1200 Newcastle-Stewart's Lane empty stock working. Little has changed at the station since the view already seen here on 14 August 1982, apart from the appearance of a car park on the left. Bearing in mind the identity of the photographer, note the very appropriate headcode in both images! *Colin J. Marsden*

▼ 28 March

I don't know how much it cost the photographer to bribe BR to set up this shot, but the chances of it happening while he was perched on a signal post in this inclement weather must have been millions to one! And how many of us, I wonder, would have even ventured up to this vantage point in the pouring rain in the first place? Whatever, he has created an incredibly imaginative shot and excelled to retain some creditable depth-of-field at f2! No 33113 is in action again, propelling 4TC set No 409 under Battledown Flyover at Worting Junction, forming the 1310 Salisbury-Waterloo service, while two 4VEPs speed in opposite directions as the 1242 Waterloo-Bournemouth (foreground) and 1212 service for the metropolis. *Brian Morrison*

▲ 1 April

The more common view of Camden Bank is of steam locomotives working hard out of Euston, with generous clouds of exhaust evidencing their efforts, but here the combined elements of electricity and running down the gradient give no such satisfying impression. Instead, the interest is in taking a last look at the Class 501s before their approaching demise, with a satisfying use of overhead gantry and cables to fill the void of the evenly lit sky. No 501159, with M61159 leading, approaches its destination as the 1205 Watford Junction-Euston stopping service, with just 18 months of life left. Like so much 'redundant' stock already seen in this volume, this coach was summarily despatched by Vic Berry in July 1986. *Brian Morrison*

▼ 21 April

While Skegness, Great Yarmouth and one or two other East Coast holiday destinations have retained their rail links and the attention of enthusiasts/photographers, Lowestoft has not been so blessed. The rail link has survived – in depleted form from days of yore – but published photographs in modern times are almost as rare as the proverbial hens' teeth! Perhaps the lack of real architectural merit is to blame, combined with the lack of glamorous motive power/trains using the station, but the photographer has done his best to create a worthwhile image. The DMU set forming the 1052 service from Ipswich has just arrived and the healthy number of travellers on this Saturday morning bodes well for the service. Note the availability of water on the platform on the left. *Ray Ruffell*

24 April

Another well thought-out and carefully composed picture, once more highlighting the benefit of 'standing back' – normally a closed gate would be both a literal and metaphorical bar to the viewer, but the slender metal tubing does not detract as much as a more substantial wooden one might. An unidentified Class 45 'Peak', perfectly positioned within the arboreal framing, crosses the graceful and delicate-looking Moorswater Viaduct at Liskeard with an up passenger service out of Penzance. Note the pillared remains of the earlier timber structure on the right. *Tom Heavyside*

▲ 25 April

In the first of two views of Class 56s on different duties, No 56034, passing 'sister' loco No 56034, approaches its destination at Eastleigh with the 1056 driver-training run from Basingstoke. Note the use of withdrawn 4SUB sets Nos 4670, 4680 and 4742 behind, giving the trainee driver a 12-coach train to play with! Fresh from Doncaster Works on 25 August 1977, the fourth of the class to be built there, No 56034 was initially allocated to Toton depot. Un-named here, it later became *Castell Ogwr/Ogmore Castle* at Bridgend on 5 June 1985. The class survived 20 years of service relatively unscathed, but withdrawals from service began in earnest as the 20th century closed. *Colin Marsden*

▼ 3 May

Double-headed this time, the need for two engines, even Type 5s with their greater haulage capacity, can be seen drawn out behind them. Although the 1020 Purfleet-Westbury train passing West Ealing is comprised of empties, the return working will be a much stiffer test for the duo. No 56043 (new in March 1978) leads No 56040 (February 1978); both initially allocated to Toton, '43 remained anonymous into 2004, whereas its 'sister' was graced with the *Oystermouth* nameplate seen on its bodyside here, at Swansea on 25 March 1982. Sadly, it was stripped of the name within a decade. *Colin Marsden*

▲ 12 May

As has already been seen, London's waste was shipped by rail to help fill former brickworks excavations at Calvert in the wilds of Buckinghamshire, north of Aylesbury. The trains were a daily ritual and a regular sight through Aylesbury station. On this day an unidentified Class 45 'Peak' waits for a clear signal to leave the Princes Risborough branch, clearly in sight of the man in the 1908-vintage Aylesbury South box. Withdrawn from service with the elimination of semaphores in the area later in the decade, the former GCR 55-lever box was preserved and transferred – most appropriately – to Swithland yard on the present-day preserved Great Central Railway. *MJS*

▼ 23 May

The range of duties allocated to and adequately handled by 'Brush 2s' became much depleted during the 1980s, and one diagram that was taken away from them was the trans-Pennine service to and from Manchester. Standing looking very clean and presentable inside Piccadilly's superb trainshed is No 31429, waiting to form the 1341 to Hull. Originally D5699, fresh from Brush on 22 April 1961 and despatched to work from Stratford shed in east London, it remained working throughout East Anglia for the next decade. Becoming No 31269 under TOPS in February 1974, it was initially withdrawn, from March depot, on 3 May 1981. Re-instated just nine months before this view, its identity changed again, to No 31429, on 16 November 1983. Final withdrawal came at Crewe Diesel Depot on 5 December 1991, and it was cut up at Booth-Roe's yard in Rotherham on 20 May 1994. *Tom Heavyside*

▲ 24 May

A strategic placing of the unit on the 'golden third', situated between balancing slabs of modern architecture, but with the attractive period design of the Refuge building in the background and the light picking out the overhead cables helping to lead the eye into the picture, the whole becomes a most satisfactory pictorial portrait of yet another ageing unit. Seen on the approach to the Manchester (Piccadilly) stop, EMU No 304010 – with M75504 leading – was one of a type that was to vanish within just a few years, especially on this route from Altrincham. This particular unit disappeared from the scene in May 1986. *Tom Heavyside*

▼ 7 June

This is yet another scene that cannot be re-created, not just because of the disappearance of the Class 50, but also due to the radical re-think of the terminal area at Paddington. The buffer-stop concourse, seen here, has changed out of all recognition and, despite the best efforts of the designers, the whole station has a much gloomier atmosphere. Showing off the class's 'large body logo' to advantage, No 50004 *St Vincent* rests at the terminus after bringing an express service from the West. Entering service in December 1967, the former D404 spent most of its life on the WR, allocated to Laira, after its removal from the WCML. Later it would receive naval crests above the nameplate, but sadly suffered from and succumbed to problems during early 1990 and languished at Laira for several months before being condemned on 22 June of that year. It was another engine to travel to Rotherham to spend time at Booth-Roe's scrapyard. *MJS*

7 June

The Victorians were renowned for making great statements with their stations, especially capital city termini. Broad Street was no exception, this magnificent edifice being both a defiant glove thrown down to its close neighbour Liverpool Street and a proud boast to all and sundry that the railway had arrived! Built in 1865 by the North London Railway on a spur from Dalston Junction, to ease the company's access to this part of the city, its boldness was initially justified, as within two years many of the NLR's 16 million annual passengers were using this facility. The platforms were well above street level and in this view, our third and final visit to Broad Street, access was by the side stairs (nearest the camera), the 1890 glazed footbridge being disused.

When electrification came to the station in 1916, only the five 'western' platforms – those seen in the second photograph – were energised. In latter years they were the only ones in use, and by the time of this photograph only four of them saw any regular traffic. Unit No 501183, on the left, draws to a halt with the 1045 stopper from Richmond.

Turning through nearly 180 degrees and looking north, we see the station 'throat' and the line towards Dalston Junction. Indicating the height of the line above its neighbours, it passed over Pindar Street and Primrose Street shortly after negotiating the curve ahead, whereas the Liverpool Street tracks went beneath them! On

the left, No 501159 stands idle between duties, while on the right No 501186 has the 'right away' for its run as the 1114 stopper to Richmond. *All MJS*

10 July

These two Class 50s are showing off their bulk and power in their 'large body logo' livery – the subsequent Network SouthEast coat never quite gave them the same sense of sheer muscle. The driver of No 50043 *Eagle*, double-heading No 50011 *Centurion*, looks back – perhaps appreciating the duo's impersonation of steam? – as the pair take up the strain to start the 1200

Penzance-Glasgow parcels train away from a pick-up stop at Bodmin Parkway (the former Bodmin Road). *Centurion* achieved notoriety as being the first of the class to be withdrawn, on 20 February 1987, a victim of accumulated TOPS hours of 8000-plus, a transfer of repairs from Crewe to Doncaster, and the need for a static test bed for '50' power units. Interestingly, it worked to its deathbed at the head of the 1S15 1215 Penzance-Glasgow as far as Crewe! *Brian Morrison*

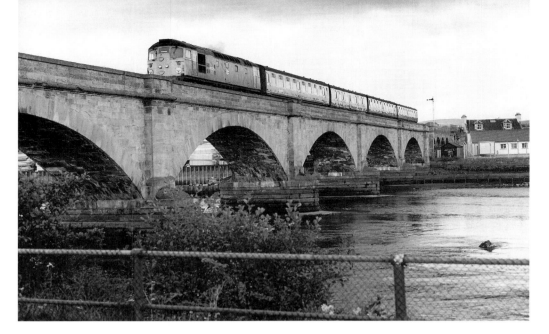

▲ 13 July

The Ness Viaduct, in Inverness, will never look the same – nor will it see this motive power again. At around 0830 on the morning of 7 February 1989 the arch seen here under the locomotive, together with the one to its right, was swept away in a raging torrent of water in the swollen river. Ten hours later, the one to their right also went under, and by midnight only the far arch survived. Needless to say, it massively disrupted services, cutting off lines north of Inverness, where stock and locomotives were stranded, and it was many months before a replacement structure was in place. That is in the future as No 26035 heads the 1755 Kyle of Lochalsh service out of Inverness. *Tom Noble*

▼ 26 July

During the 1980s there was only one loco-hauled train diagrammed to run over the Paddington-Wolverhampton route that had once been the GWR's express way to the capital from Birkenhead and home to 'Kings' roaring services south in competition with the LMS's WCML. The 0822 from Wolverhampton returned north as the 1740 from Paddington and was for many years rostered for Class 50 haulage. The latter service is seen bathed in a weak early evening sun as No 50043 *Eagle* (seen opposite) begins to slow for the Beaconsfield stop. Withdrawn on 1 February 1991, *Eagle* was sold to the 16CVST Group at Birmingham Railway Museum. Sadly, restoration was not to come and the loco was moved to the private Pontypool & Blaenavon Railway, on whose site it was finally cut up by the end of 2001. *MJS*

17 July

One of the most interesting – and spectacular – events of the decade was the specially staged demonstration test collision with a nuclear flask. Organised by the CEGB at Old Dalby, to show the safety properties of its flasks, it was televised for those millions who were not invited to the actual event. Like that unhappy majority, I could only witness the mayhem through my TV screen and, although dramatic, the true nature of the event on the ground could only be guessed at. Thus No

46009 carved its place in history, by being the only diesel locomotive to achieve its demise in this fashion! In these two views, the photographer has superbly captured the moment of impact – with the 'Peak' literally ploughing (unmanned!) into the waiting flask at 100mph and the Mk 1 coach behind it beginning to buckle – and its immediate aftermath. Amidst the smoke, a coach bogie rears into the air. The flask was intact, but how much safer did the general public really feel?
Both Colin Marsden

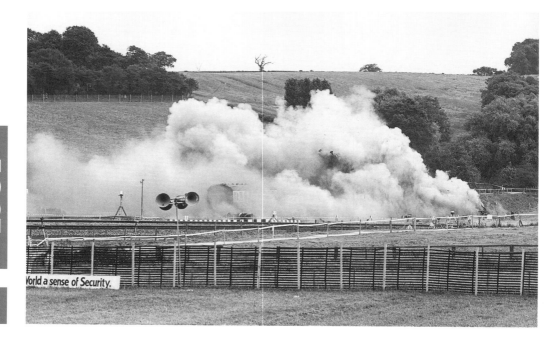

▲ 29 July

During the 1990s, the former diesel/DMU servicing shed situated next to Buxton station was taken out of use, with the locomotives being stabled at Great Rocks instead. Thus sights like this at the end of the day at that shed could no longer be enjoyed. Banned from entrance to the building at this time, No 47124 stands on the left, in company with Nos 37196 and 37120. The 'Brush 4' was new in February 1964 as D1714 – working from Old Oak Common and helping to eliminate much-loved ex-GWR classes – and was another to finish life in Glasgow, at MC Metals, being cut up by 24 October 1990. The '37s' had started life as D6896 and D6820, in April 1964 and March 1963 respectively, and both were still officially 'on the books' into 2004. Both, too, were graced with names, the former becoming *Tre Pol and Pen* at Truro on 16 July 1985 and the latter (as No 37887) *Castell Caerffili/Caerphilly Castle*. *MJS*

▼ 31 July

Two days later, the light is escaping again. The proximity of the stabled locomotives can be seen on the extreme right, with No 20191 visible, as two varying types of DMU stand in the station between duties. On the left is a Class 108 unit, while the main object of interest is BRCW Class 104 set BX481, with DMCL M53487 leading. Built in July 1957, it saw withdrawal in May 1989 and cutting at Vic Berry's yard in December 1990. *MJS*

▲ 1 August

Throughout the decade there were many anniversaries and attendant celebrations, which seemed to crop up with amazing regularity! One that was slightly out of the ordinary was the 150th anniversary of Wilsons Brewery in the North West. A number of runs were made by preserved Webb 'Coal Tank' No 1054, radiating from Manchester (Victoria), into which station it is seen arriving bunker-first, while another Class 104 DMU tries to catch up. Built at Crewe in 1888, one of 300 built for the LNWR, No 1054 assumed the number 7799 under the LMS and, finally, 58926 post-Nationalisation. Withdrawn from Bletchley shed in November 1958, it escaped the cutter's torch to be saved for the nation and latterly has enjoyed the Keighley & Worth Valley Railway as home. *MJS*

▼ 1 August

On the same day more mundane fare was also at hand, in the guise of a Class 108 (left) and No 31213 (right). Standing in a spare through road at Victoria, the 'Brush 2' is acting as station pilot, providing back-up should any be needed. New as D5637 on 28 July 1960 at Stratford, it became No 31465 on 25 February 1985, 31565 on 17 August 1990, then back to 31465 on 7 February 1993. Initially withdrawn, from Bescot, on 16 February 1999, it was re-instated 11 days later and was still officially listed in 2004. *MJS*

1 August

Still in Manchester, 'Whistler' No 40091 makes one of its very last trips, past Piccadilly station on its way to Longsight depot and withdrawal one month and one day later. Towed on to the main line for the short trip to the depot by a twin-car DMU, it is devoid of crew and life. Note the two differing styles of 'unofficial' numbers on the nose-end and the attempt at giving it an 'e' number! Fresh out of the nearby Vulcan Foundry on 29 August 1960, as D290, it was a WCML engine throughout, beginning at Crewe North shed and finishing at Longsight. *MJS*

1984

117

10 August

Although limited in number compared to the two alternative types, dual-powered diesel/electric locomotives and units had a real advantage if there were power failures or electrified services were forced on to non-electrified routes. Like all types of motive power, however, they were not without misfortune, and due to arcing problems that had caused No 73142 *Broadlands* to burn out, some Gatwick-Victoria trains at this time were worked on diesel power alone. Nos 73111 and 73117 (later named *University of Surrey* at Waterloo on 3 July 1987) power the 1115 airport express past East Croydon. No 73111 was withdrawn on 30 May 1991, whereas its 'sister' was still around in 2004, surviving a withdrawal in January 1999, to be re-instated on 14 May 2003. *Brian Morrison*

▲ 11 August
Back at Buxton, a rare visitor at this time is snapped entering the station stabling point, having finished its duties for the time being in the Great Rocks area. Many of the 'Rats' had already gone by this time, but there were a number that were soldiering on, usually handling 'second-division' duties. No 25191 began life as D7541 on 29 March 1965 at Nottingham; after a move to Cricklewood shed that October, it was transferred to Longsight on 25 May 1968, as part of the fleet to handle the final withdrawal of steam. The WCML remained its home thereafter, final withdrawal coming on 18 March 1987 from Crewe Diesel Depot. Thankfully, preservation beckoned and the locomotive became based at the North Yorks Moors Railway, where it acquired the name *The Diana. MJS*

▼ 11 August
While I was enjoying the weather at Buxton, this photographer was also bathed in sunshine, although somewhat further north. At Wennington, on the former MR route from Hellifield to Lancaster, No 31440 hauls its five-coach load past the 1890-built, 27-lever, typically Midland Wennington Junction box. So named because of the Furness & Midland Joint branch that once struck out north-west at this point, there is no longer a junction to negotiate by this 1336 Lancaster-Hull service. *Tom Heavyside*

August

One more example of why Brian Morrison is a successful professional photographer. Putting the signal box in the dominant foreground position, with the HST and the branch playing second fiddle, is the masterstroke – far from overpowering or detracting, the added interest, especially the glimpse of the signalman, holds the eye. The exhaust of power car No 43138 in the heat of the day indicates some hard work as it approaches Clink Road Junction box, Frome, with the 1250 Plymouth-Paddington express. Sadly, this view cannot be replicated, as the box has now gone; this factor alone, aside from the skilful composition, reinforces the message that one should photograph everything and anything, as they could disappear before you know it! *Brian Morrison*

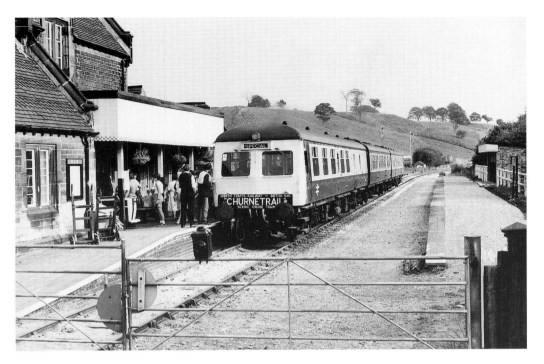

▲ 27 August

The former North Staffordshire Railway station at Cheddleton closed, together with all the others on the branch from Uttoxeter through Leek, on 4 January 1965. Amazingly, and seemingly against all odds, the route remained linked and even received some publicity, as seen with this 'Scenic Cruise Train' at the site headed by Swindon Class 120 DMBC No 53706 on a special from Stoke. New in November 1957, as one of the early orders for DMUs to replace steam, it survived until December 1986, after which it was yet another to make the trip to Leicester and Vic Berry's scrapyard by June 1987. This 'North Staffs Railway/British Rail' 'Churnet Trail' tour has obviously picked a good day to transport its healthy complement of passengers along the route, and no doubt some of them have become stalwart supporters of the new Churnet Valley Railway, based at this station. *Tom Heavyside*

▼ 31 August

A take-over by 'Grids' at Westbury! Certainly there is not much in the way of variety of motive power here, but a healthy amount of freight. Nos 56048 and 56039 swing round the curve double-headed on the approach to the station with the 1020 Purfleet-Merehead empties, while left and right Nos 56047 and 56034 temporarily take a back seat, awaiting their turn for the road. *Colin Marsden*

▲ 30 August

A retrospective look at the 1980s can become a liturgy of things that have gone, so many of them for ever. Like so many of its contemporaries, this siding is one that has been dispensed with. On this day, however, 'Crompton' No 33052 has a very healthy consist and the guard hangs from the window to keep an eye on things as the driver opens the regulator to move the heavy load up the gradient from British Industrial Sand at Holmethorpe yard, to run just a mile or so to Redhill yard. *Colin Marsden*

▼ 1 September

Another '33', this time on a route away from its normal home territory: No 33031 heads north on the single track from Yeovil, at Cockhill near Castle Cary, with the 1020 Weymouth-Cardiff 'Severn-Solent' service. Prior to the introduction of 'Sprinters', the 'Cromptons' gave enthusiasts along the line and at Bristol a welcome variety of motive power. *Colin Marsden*

3 September

A closely observed train! Providing an interesting comparison of motive power, a cyclist has come to the station and rests with his arms across his handlebars, patiently waiting for his train to arrive and viewing No 43127 leading a Bristol-bound express at speed through Taplow station. Unnamed for more than 20 years as just one of the 197 HST power cars, No 43127 was given the honour at Old Oak Common on 17 September 2003, becoming *Sir Peter Parker 1924-2002. Cotswold Line 150.*

Taplow also provides another look at the bulk of the Class 50s, slightly exaggerated by the near-front zoomed aspect. Roaring through the station on its way to London, No 50038 *Formidable* is living up to its name on an 'extra' rake of eight Mk 1s. New from Vulcan Foundry in September 1968, as D438, *Formidable* received its name at Laira on 5 May 1978. Thereafter it plied along the WR main lines until the run-down of the class and its final withdrawal on 27 September 1988 from Old Oak Common. It was yet another item of stock to be cut at Vic Berry's yard. *Both MJS*

30 September

Mention of Vic Berry's Leicester scrapyard leads neatly to this picture, of rare visitors Nos 82004 and 82006 at Leicester's ex-MR shed site, resting before their final trip. These two electrics had emerged from Beyer Peacock's Manchester Works within three months of each other – as E3050 and E3052, in September and December 1960 – then proceeded to give more than 20 years of unsung effort on the WCML, gradually being relegated to lesser duties after the arrival of the Class 87s in the mid-1970s. The end came in October and July 1983 respectively, and Vic Berry had completely reduced them to nothing within days of this view.

While not a part of BR, Vic Berry's yard might well have been so, considering the amount of ex-BR stock that passed through! This is the yard in its heyday, with shunter No 03069 on the left, resting at the weekend between duties, and Park Royal Class 103 DTCL No M56050 still clinging tenaciously to its bogies! New in September 1959 from Doncaster Works as D2069 and allocated to West Hartlepool, the diminutive shunter stayed in the North East throughout its working life on BR, finally giving up the ghost at Gateshead on 27 November 1983. Quickly snapped up by Vic Berry for use in his yard, it was made redundant when the yard was destroyed by fire, and was sold to the Gloucestershire/Warwickshire Railway Society in August 1991. *Both MJS*

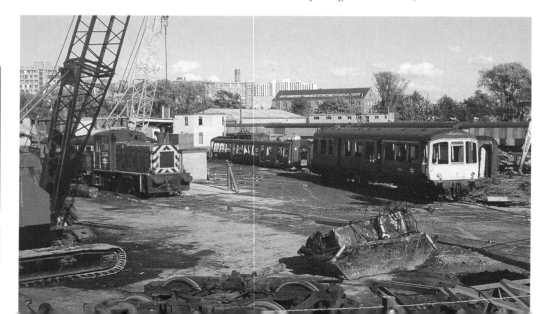

21 October
Choice of vantage point, 'painting' with light and making strategic use of its direction (the 90° angle and low position picking out every possible projection and indentation) transform this otherwise uninspiring view of two Class 501 units in Watford Junction, helped by with the inclusion of the human interest and the hand-made 'Not This Train' notice. Nos 501170 (left and 501148 rest as empty stock between duties, captured on a 400 ASA film, taken with a 1/60th second shutter set at f11. *MJS*

2 November

The water looks cold on this late-autumn day, even despite the bright sun. My only visit to Stranraer was in steam days, as one of a party of four teenagers touring Scotland in my ageing 'sit-up-and-beg' Ford Popular, and it was bitterly cold then! That was long before the direct line from Carlisle was severed west of Dumfries and all traffic was forced to travel via Ayr. Somehow, rail links have survived, not least to the ferries, despite all odds and the constant mantra of BR to cut back services to save money. Here No 08591 shunts empty car carriers and an oil tank near the loading bay at Stranraer Harbour, years before there were moves to re-open the direct link. *Tom Heavyside*

4 November

Following the rare sight of the two Class 82s, their rarity was undermined by the arrival at Vic Berry's yard of a stream of '83s'! Left to right, they are Nos 83001, 83007, 83010 and 83002, all awaiting their fate under leaden skies, but all apparently in good shape. All of them new in 1960 – 83001 as E3024 and the rest numbered consecutively – they went about their business without fuss and all but two of the class made it into the 1980s; these four were withdrawn en bloc on 17 July 1983, together with most of the rest of the class. All had gone between December 1984 and January 1985.

Despite being the youngest of the crowd gathered at the yard, No 83011 was the first to go and is seen here with just the two cabs and the barest of framing remaining – an indignity for a once proud servant of BR. No 83011 was new from English Electric's Vulcan Foundry on 30 January 1961, with the initial allocation of 'ACL', being the overall notation for 'AC Lines' and covering the WCML electrified route. Eventually this collective term was abandoned, with specific depots again regaining allocation. The end came for this locomotive at Longsight, on 17 July, together with its brethren seen above. *Both MJS*

Index